FACING THE LION

HOW TO COPE

WITH
MISUNDERSTANDING,
INJUSTICE, AND
SUFFERING

every blessing

Pamela Mack

FACING THE LION

HOW TO COPE
WITH
MISUNDERSTANDING, INJUSTICE, AND SUFFERING

A *True-Life Story*
by Pamela Vack

WINEPRESS WP PUBLISHING

Packaged by WinePress Publishing, PO Box 428, Enumclaw, WA 98022. The views expressed or implied in this work do not necessarily reflect those of WinePress Publishing. Ultimate design, content, and editorial accuracy of this work are the responsibilities of the author.

ISBN 1-57921-325-1
Library of Congress Catalog Card Number: 00-107710

Acknowledgments

Special thanks to Hector, my God-given husband, for his patience and continual encouragement. To dear Frida Harris and Juliet Hughes of the Fellowship of Christian Writers' Association for all their loving support and much needed inspiration toward publication, and to Alan Levett for his initial help and advice.

I thank God for you all, and to Him be the glory!

Objectives

This book will encourage and inspire Christians, particularly disabled women, who find themselves struggling against illness and handicap and asking the question, Why? Pamela Vack does not offer simplistic answers to the perennial question of why God allows suffering. Through her own testimony, she demonstrates how the love of God can work in a Christian disciple to overcome the stalking "lion" of illness, renewing a person inwardly, even though her outward being is wasting away.

Pamela Vack offers new insights into a little-known motor neuron disease and catalogues her struggles to convince the medical profession that something is organically wrong. Specialists seem to refuse to believe or help her, though the final diagnosis includes many illnesses overlaying each other. Her case may be unique, but the struggles will be familiar to many.

The book follows her trail of trying to prove vaccine damage, topical in the light of recent claims about inoculations and biological damage in the Gulf War. There is no happy ending; her condition is worsening, and she has vaccination-caused immune system breakdown.

Running through the book is a love story—her love for her husband and her love for God. Her husband, Hector, is always there, supporting her when no one else believes her. Together their love and trust in God keeps them pressing on and looking beyond themselves. It is a story of victory over circumstances because the participants follow God's way.

Contents

. . . Your enemy the devil prowls around like a roaring lion looking for someone to devour. Resist him, standing firm in the faith, because you know that your brothers throughout the world are undergoing the same kind of sufferings. (1 Peter 5:8)

Preface

What is the reason for illness? Is it just physical, mental, or what? Why does God allow His people to suffer illness? The perennial question. . . . There are many reasons; this book will not attempt to deal with them all. One answer is provided in the story of Job: Whenever God's people suffer as Job did, in whole or in part, what is revealed in Heaven about him can also be applied to our lives. The following true story ably shows this as the writer details the very searching and extensive trials through which she passed. They contain much that shows the spiritual warfare in which she was—and still is—engaged in as a Christian (Eph. 6:12).

In 2 Corinthians 10:4, the apostle Paul writes: "The weapons we fight with are not the weapons of the world. On the contrary, they have divine power to demolish strongholds." He goes on to explain that it is our thoughts which are taken captive. In Christ, we reverse the fate of Eve, who lost the argument with the devil, and we gain victories of the mind against all that Hell can throw against us.

The story that follows illustrates how God can use a suffering instrument, supported by the power of faith, to resist the devil's power and to win the argument. Our Christian witness is not just to the world of men and women, but also to the unseen world. God could destroy with a stroke of His own almighty strength the whole power of darkness, but He has chosen the weak things of the world to confound the things that are mighty.

Who can tell the extent by which God's people, willingly used by God at times of suffering in their lives, have protected others too weak to stand? Through their endurance in battle, they have driven back in confusion the enemies of God.

ALAN LEVETT

Chapter One

Second Chance

IF ONLY I HAD BEEN ABLE TO CATCH A GLIMPSE TEN YEARS AGO OF ALL that was in store for me, I wonder what my response would have been? To be given a fresh opportunity for a real commitment to follow Jesus Christ, to experience God's precious love and joy, to know the discipline of hard and painful trials, to suffer physically and emotionally. . . .

Would I have been willing to learn how to rejoice in suffering, a lesson I have to learn continually? But what about the joy of being totally forgiven? I would not have missed that! What freedom from guilt to live daily in the realization that Jesus died for me and took all my sin upon Himself. What a joy to know Him personally!

It's been good to look back through those ten eventful years knowing God's hand was firmly upon me through many experiences that I know now He has allowed for my good, all in accordance with His purposes.

It was during the year of 1979 that I first sensed something happening. I saw the Holy Spirit at work, though I didn't realize it at first. I witnessed a change in the lives of some close friends, then my younger daughter, who was still at school, was led by a boyfriend into a charismatic church. She began telling my husband, Hector, and me about "gifts" in the church, people who prophesied, those who had a gift of healing.

Hector and I were concerned. What did it all mean? I am thankful looking back, that we didn't dismiss it all but had a desire to find out more for ourselves, especially as we saw the evidence of a kind of transforming power in the lives of people around us. We had been happily married for eight years (Hector was my second husband), and we thought we had all we needed, but change was to come.

In my teens I had made a commitment to follow God, but had lapsed in it, and then I found myself in the experience of a wrong marriage and all its distressing consequences over a fourteen year period, nevertheless the blessing of two lovely daughters. Marriage to Hector, a lapsed Catholic, in 1972, found me in search of real meaning to life and a longing to be free from a heavy sense of guilt. Having gone my own way and justified my own sinful actions and decisions during the previous marriage and thereafter, my heart and soul were at last prepared to seek forgiveness and restoration in my relationship with God. How good it would be to have a second chance!

It was during a moving service of baptism at my former church, listening to a close friend give her testimony of faith and watching her step into the water to be baptized, that I felt my heart and spirit being challenged.

"*You* should be down there being baptized!" the Spirit of God seemed to be saying to me. "Are you now prepared?"

During the weeks of autumn 1979, I watched and noted the changes in my daughter, and eventually attended her church in Corfe Mullen with my husband Hector. How good it felt to be prayed for, to ask God for forgiveness, and to make a wholehearted recommitment. When I once again became involved in church, my husband was continually challenged.

"Darling, I'm so happy for you," Hector would say. "Going back to church is obviously important to you, and I can see you're enjoying it. But please understand my own feelings. I've only ever known Roman Catholic dogma, and I'm not ready to consider any other way at the moment."

He added that he didn't know God in a personal way as I did, because he had only ever believed that God "lived" in the church building he went to on a Sunday morning. The idea that the Holy Spirit could live in him was something quite new to Hector. I began to understand his thinking and background and realized his difficulties.

I loved him so much. I thanked God for giving me a second chance in marriage. Here I was with a dark, attractive partner of Italian extraction. Hector had the kindest eyes, often with a glint of humor, a good head of nearly black hair, and a beard to match. I did my best to keep both hair and beard in reasonable shape! We were approximately the same height, if I remembered not to wear the stiletto heels that I'd been so fond of. Out of consideration for him, I switched to "flatties," so much better for my feet and posture!

Hector's warmth and affection matched my own needs. His humor, gentleness, and thoughtfulness were great blessings, and somehow we seemed to have that complete rapport, physically and emotionally. How much more precious that oneness would be if we were united in the Lord!

I became anxious and apprehensive over my new commitment, because I was zealous to talk about it and longed to share it all with Hector.

"Lord, don't let it be a wedge between us," I prayed. My friends in the Free Church also prayed, and one Sunday I left my Bible open on the kitchen table where I knew he would see it and went off to church feeling something was about to happen.

When I arrived home Hector was waiting for me.

"Hello, darling!" he said brightly. "I've been really absorbed while you've been out. I've just finished reading these passages. I couldn't put it down." He had been reading the whole of the last book of the Bible—the Revelation!

I stared at him as he carried on enthusiastically. "I never realized how relevant the Scriptures are for today. And how challenging they are, personally. I've never been encouraged to read the Bible before, I suppose."

With a lump in my throat, I said: "Oh, I'm really glad you found it so interesting."

God had heard our prayers. Hector was hungry for answers, and he felt he had a lot of sorting out to do. He started going to local Roman Catholic churches and finally decided his place was with me in the Free Evangelical Church.

Some months later, in 1980, we were both baptized, along with my daughter, on our wedding anniversary, too. It was unforgettable. I had the opportunity to give my testimony and speak about God's love and grace in my life and the second chance to follow Him. The Lord is good and faithful.

Becoming a Christian didn't mean we were promised an easy, trouble-free life. We were to discover that through all life's problems, God was always with us, upholding, guiding, and meeting every need. Learning to trust God for the next step, we grew in our faith as we experienced first hand how "in all things God works for the good of those who love Him, who have been called according to his purpose" (Rom. 8:29).

It wasn't long before our new faith was tested.

Our accountant had let us down badly. All the company books had to be examined, going back many years, and there was a large tax bill involving possible penalties and insurmountable problems. Financially, everything looked very bleak, and we faced the possibility of having to sell our lovely home. How we prayed. I had to reach the point where I was willing to let the house go, then loaded down with particulars of smaller houses and other accommodation from estate agents, we wondered what to do. Then new accountants advised us to place our house in a company, or corporation within my husbands' business, which thankfully, and quite miraculously, enabled us to pay the necessary tax bills over six years. A hard lesson in trust!

Through the Free Evangelical Church, we joined a house church, which outgrew the home we met in. Our next place of worship was a day center that could hold 100 people, and this too grew. These were exciting days for us, and we wanted to share the "Good News" with everyone we met, but we could see our families and friends were suspicious and wondering why we had become fervent Christians. Our eager talk about Jesus Christ was met with indifference and unbelief; others seemed to feel safer with the "old" Pam and Hector. So we had to learn patience and the practice of intercessory prayer for others. Only the Holy Spirit could change hearts.

I valued the experience of being a volunteer with the Samaritans (a national helpline for the despairing and suicidal), listening and getting alongside those who had little hope, motivation or will to live, young and old, for whom sheer loneliness resulted in depression and hopelessness. Frequently, as a last resort, I would offer to pray for them, and this was gratefully accepted, though it was unofficial. I enjoyed my weekly duties, working in shifts within a team. I did it for nearly ten years, not understanding at the time that this was all in God's plan, and that He was preparing me for new ministry later. It was sobering to listen to battered wives, confused children, drug addicts, and alcoholics who lived rough lives and who had lost any meaning or hope. Comforting them in their distress at the centre, where they were encouraged to call or telephone made me thankful for my marriage, home, good friends, and family love.

I remember taking for granted the wonderful gift of good health and the possession of tremendous energy. As a member of a tennis club, I enjoyed regular games of tennis, badminton, and, later, squash, while learning a few deceptive shots to slow down my younger opponents. I had mild spondylosis, which I'd had since my twenties, but it was manageable, and it didn't hinder long walks or my sporting activities.

Our lovely home became "open house," and we asked the Lord to give us the gift of hospitality, one of the spiritual gifts mentioned in the Bible. He certainly answered our prayers; more and more people with problems or who simply wanted fellowship would pop in spontaneously. We found these times such an encouragement to us, and it was a privilege to be used in this way.

When my two daughters left the nest, after taking A-level exams to continue their education at university and polytechnic, I missed them very much, but Hector and I found we had more time for each other and for others.

We both loved traveling and exploring, so we enjoyed frequent holidays abroad, particularly to the south of France in September and May, and to a little apartment in the Canary Islands for a few weeks in the sun during England's cold winter months.

Several people in our church who were in need of a break were able to use our little havens abroad; they came back refreshed, with stories of their adventures to share.

When we look back now we are amazed at what God has done. I find it hard to believe that just over ten years ago we were threatened with what felt like a forty-foot tidal wave—complete financial ruin. Yet by God's grace that was overcome. We learned that He would meet our every need and more. In numerous ways we could see that the Lord was directing our paths and going before us, teaching us to trust Him, and to know that His ways are best and His timing perfect.

Looking at my younger daughter, Caroline, we could see God at work. She had begun life rather traumatically ten months after the crib death of my baby son in 1964. Three times in her first three years, she narrowly escaped death. On the first occasion, at about four weeks old, she suffered double regurgitation and near-suffocation. Almost blue, she was rushed to hospital where the obstruction was removed and she could breathe again—but only just in time.

Then she fell into a small swimming pool and floated face down, much to the amazement of her elder sister, Sheri, who was about to congratulate her on her swimming ability, when she realized something was wrong. Hauled out and given the breath of life once again, she didn't give us long to recover before we had further panic and more gray hairs.

While spending a holiday in our Mudeford beach hut, we noticed she could not seem to shake off the remnants of a cold. Gradually it turned to pneumonia, and she was once again rushed into hospital. After numerous injections and close medical care, she was brought through again.

During these anxious episodes, I often wondered whether she would be taken from me, too, like the tragic loss of my little baby son. Psychologically, I almost prepared myself to face her loss and watched over her very protectively. But Someone else was protecting her. Now we could see God's hand on her, keeping her safe and bringing her to faith in Him, and then using her as an instrument to bring her mother, and eventually her stepfather, into that new life a Christian enjoys.

But that new life was going to be severely tested and subjected to misunderstandings and those valley experiences through which we learn to trust.

I would discover that it is in the deepest valleys that the sweetest fruit grows.

Chapter Two

Trusting

AS THE YEARS MOVED ON, WE LIVED OUR LIVES TO THE FULL, TRUST-
ing God to see us through the repayment of the back tax
bill which would take us six years to achieve. Hector and I
looked forward to enjoying some warmth and sunshine at
a small apartment we had bought in Gran Canary. It was
something good to look forward to in our cold and bleak
English winters! The first people to use it were a young
family in our church.

The winter months of 1986 were drawing near, and
Hector and I considered the possibility of our first holiday
in our "little haven in the sun." However, it was not to be.
Our way was blocked, as our apartment was under con-
tract with the administrator for letting all the winter months.
Having decided the door was firmly closed in that direction, we were recommended to visit The Gambia and enjoy
its beautiful climate and superb beaches. That seemed an
excellent idea, and, eventually, we made the necessary plans
for the flight and accommodation.

How exciting to have the chance to visit Africa! We were thrilled, and thanked God for providing the necessary money. We would use it as an opportunity to take Bibles and Christian literature to a people living where superstition was rife.

It was recommended we both have the necessary injections: yellow fever, typhoid, and tetanus, plus the polio blob on a lump of sugar!

It took a few weeks for the formalities to be completed, and then we were ready for our month-long December holiday.

Our cases were full of shorts, tops, swim wear galore, and tennis gear. More importantly to us, we had a pack of Bibles, leaflets, and New Testaments to give away. We trusted that the Lord would direct us to people who needed them.

Within twenty-four hours, we found ourselves in a hotel room enjoying fellowship with three black Moslems, who told us they were longing to hear the gospel of Christ! We were so encouraged and knew that God had indeed gone before and prepared the way. What a busy time we had, involving ourselves with The Church of Christ, in the savannah amidst the basic shanty villages and compounds. It was dusty, hot, and different from any holiday we had ever experienced before; it was certainly a culture shock for us and a sobering experience.

But we loved every minute of it, cycling with no springs in the saddles along dusty, pot-holed roads into the villages. Frequently I gave up attempting to cycle. Hector rode on, but for me it was less painful to walk, particularly as the children loved to thrust a bamboo stick into the spokes of the bicycles while we were moving. I didn't think that was funny!

We had the opportunity to go into the compounds and meet some of the beautiful Gambians and their families. Some had never met white people before, and we observed an old lady who moved out of her round mud-and-wattle house and waved a voodoo stick in order to cast away evil spirits. We reached out to these people in the love and peace of our Lord and had many opportunities to encourage them and talk about our faith.

We will never forget a handsome teacher from Nigeria and his brother from Togo, who kindly invited us to their little bungalow for an evening meal. It was quite an experience. We enjoyed their company, and they had prepared a delicious meal for us from a local recipe. We found them interesting people to talk to, and they were open to the Gospel of Jesus Christ. In return, we invited them to our hotel for dinner, which would be among ninety-nine percent white Europeans! Would they come?

As dusk fell, we looked for their arrival at the entrance to the hotel on the beach. What a surprise we had when we spotted them; George the Nigerian was dressed "conventionally" to us, but Michael arrived in his Togo costume—very colorful and elaborate. We felt proud to be with them. All eyes were on Michael as we queued for a tasty meal of hot and cold fare, laid out on long buffet tables. Many of the stares and facial expressions from our fellow Europeans were, sadly, none too hospitable. Some looked positively angry as we entertained our new black friends.

They were four precious weeks with new experiences and a fresh awareness of the African way of life. The long sunny days spent swimming, playing tennis, and exploring were idyllic. But it was a culture shock to see how life is lived primitively for so many in The Gambia, walking miles for water, the women of the family toiling long hours in the fields. Little seemed to have changed with the passage of time, but their hand-built homes and compounds, and the closeness and protection of their family units impressed us.

We arrived home in Bournemouth feeling thankful for all the benefits we enjoyed, reminding ourselves that we had running water, warmth, and more than enough to feed and clothe ourselves. How cosseted we were! We had really enjoyed our first experience of Africa and looked forward to the possibility of returning one day. We were both tanned and feeling very fit after playing tennis every day in the cool of the evening on the hotel grounds.

So it was an unpleasant surprise to discover within three weeks of returning home that my left hand had gone quite numb, followed within another three weeks by my right hand.

Not feeling unduly anxious, but reasoning that these symptoms could be temporary and due to an old cervical disc problem, I chose to continue playing squash in the hope that normal feeling would return. The deadness refused to disappear, however, and even began to increase.

At this point I decided to ask the advice of my younger daughter, Caroline, who was at that time completing her four-year nursing degree at Surrey University and happened to be with us on one of her frequent visits home.

She suggested that I should visit my general practitioner and considered I could be developing pernicious anemia or even diabetes. I was rather appalled at that idea, but nevertheless made an appointment to see my doctor.

The day of the appointment arrived, and I crawled out of bed feeling positively "fluey" and very peculiar! My coordination was affected, and feeling somewhat lightheaded, I made my way to my GP's surgery.

I displayed my two very dead hands for him to see and explained the peculiar symptoms that were steadily developing. He patiently checked my blood pressure, balance, and so on, and quickly decided that I should be referred to a neurologist.

While waiting for the appointment with the specialist, I continued to play sport, but badly. I felt frustrated that I was losing more than winning. What was wrong? Why couldn't I hit the rapidly moving squash ball more decisively? Evident coordination problems were occurring. Meanwhile, I would have frequent bouts of feeling "drunk," and my legs were becoming numb, my left foot in particular, and this feeling was gradually moving upward.

Could this be some strange illness picked up from one of the villages in The Gambia?

My appointment with the neurologist finally came, and off I went with my husband, not knowing quite what form of examination would occur. Out came the usual tools of the trade to check reflexes and numbness, and the loathed sharp key drawn down under my feet, which were then quite ticklish. My attempts to walk an imaginary tightrope were hilarious as I fell about all over the place. The examination completed, the neurologist suggested that I could seek a second opinion, and I could "attempt to get back on the tennis court." What a joke—if only it were possible! Was he really serious?

I continued to develop various strange symptoms, adding something new to the list almost weekly. I tried hard to feel normal again.

During this time, my caring church family became concerned, and they offered to pray for me and exercise the laying on of hands for healing.

I still continued to look fairly normal on the outside—a picture of health, no doubt with a good suntan disguising a multitude of problems. Therefore, as I became worse, it was doubly hard for family and friends to take my symptoms seriously. I could see them thinking: "Oh yes, it's probably all psychosomatic. . . ."

But I went ahead with the second opinion, after which it was suggested I have a lumbar puncture, followed by some electric conduction tests. I didn't like the idea of two days in hospital, lying flat on my back, but I agreed to have the tests done, plus x-rays to check a minor cervical lesion or spondylosis, which had been with me for many years and had not really presented any lengthy problems other than needing occasional manipulation or bedrest.

Eventually, I was told during a subsequent consultation that the lumbar puncture revealed an abnormally high level of protein, and would I consider going to the London Hospital for an MRI scan?

I discussed all these details with my medically-trained daughter who told me she was beginning to consider the possibility that I had multiple sclerosis. Because of the timing of the onset of the illness, we began to look at the chances of the vaccines being the root cause. I knew that in some cases vaccinations can cause an abnormal immune response. Could that explain what was happening to my body?

Since I knew nothing about neurological illnesses, she gave me some notes on multiple sclerosis and similar diseases. Certainly, I was experiencing similar symptoms, but they seemed to be gradually affecting my whole body.

What on earth was going on? Surely I was going to bet better? Oh please, Lord, don't let me lose my good health; I couldn't bear it. . . .

Chapter Three

Perseverance

MORE AND MORE GOD WAS SHOWING ME THAT HIS TIMING IS ABSO-lutely perfect, and no experience is ever wasted, however hard it may seem at the time.

During the ten years leading up to 1986, I was privi-leged to be invited with the Samaritans as a volunteer, ready with a listening ear for people in despair or distress. We were all committed to one duty per week (and many did more), plus a night duty, thus offering a 24-hour service and help-line over the telephone, and a "flying squad" for night-time emergencies.

When the doorbell of the Center rang, we were never sure who was calling or what would be their state of mind. Some were very much under the influence of alcohol and would insist on bringing their bottle into the building (of-ten concealed initially in a carrier bag), and occasionally a caller's anger at life and circumstances would spill over into violence.

On becoming a Christian, and being convinced that in Jesus Christ dwelt the real answer to problems, I found myself naturally wanting to share my faith and offer prayer to those who were at rock bottom, having lost all hope. Even as unbelievers, there were those who welcomed being prayed for, and who were prepared to listen to the promises of Jesus, clinging to the little hope they could muster. This made me unpopular with the other volunteers, who were disturbed when I was asked to pray for clients. Eventually I was reported to the director.

I stood in his office wondering if I was going to be expelled from working with the charity. With growing boldness, I explained my faith in Jesus Christ and the reasons for wanting to encourage others who were in need of the only true Hope in life. I felt I had nothing to lose; the Holy Spirit kept me strong, and I remembered the words of the apostle Paul in the Bible: "I am not ashamed of the Gospel of Christ" (Rom. 1:16).

The director let me off with a caution: "Keep your faith outside the Samaritans!"

I continued my voluntary duties until my peculiar symptoms meant I was unable to plan ahead and book a month in advance. In our morning prayers, Hector and I prayed for direction, and the Lord was faithful in opening a new door and a fresh opportunity to be used for His glory.

We were asked to join the pastoring team in our church. As the congregation had grown in numbers, various problems among the members needed attention. There was a real necessity for more prayer and inner healing, more encouragement and deliverance. My ten year's involvement with the Samaritans was indeed valuable experience, and as we worked together, we saw the Lord bringing freedom and peace.

How much more worthwhile ministry is, when we see *evidence* of the burden of sin and guilt banished, peace restored, and all negative emotions dealt with, bringing about real trust, faith, and hope in Jesus, who promises He will never forsake us.

Hector and I were so privileged to be part of this caring team, but we realized we needed the guidance and discernment of the Holy Spirit; we could do nothing without Him!

It was indeed a joy to be working for God as part of a loving church family, but as the years of 1986 and 1987 went by, I began to dislike my body and what it was doing to me.

Week by week strange symptoms would develop. Gradually, awful fatigue caused me to rest more frequently, and paresthesia moved insidiously through my legs and into my hips. Without the precious sense of touch, odd things were happening to the muscles in my legs, and they refused to respond and work normally as I walked. Pain would set in; even a warm bath, which I thought would be comforting and bring relief, would cause me pain. Frequently feeling "drunk," I would stagger about, longing for my world to remain still, particularly during supermarket shopping, which became extremely difficult to face, as I felt threatened and unstable on my legs.

Eventually, after regular consultations with my neurologist, it was suggested that I should go into the hospital and undergo intravenous steroid treatment and intensive physiotherapy. The day arrived to settle into the Lansdowne Private Hospital for a two-week duration, believing the Lord would restore and heal through medical means.

My church family and friends promised to continue surrounding me with prayer. Words of encouragement from the Bible—verses that I still hold on to today—lifted me up daily.

I had to learn how to take one day at a time; eventually, that would become a reality, although the Enemy would occasionally place negative fears in my mind about the future. When this happened I would acknowledge these thoughts, and by an act of will, redirect them on to positive blessings and praise to God, and, thankfully, the negativity did not take root and bring me down into depression and despair. The consequence, I found, was a praising and grateful heart, for there are always things to give thanks for. The Lord is good!

All this I would learn. But for now there was some anxiety as an intravenous drip was inserted into my wrist. The steroid was certainly a form of shock treatment to my nervous system; it would possibly give me a remission, or even better, bring the relapse to a halt entirely!

My church family prayed fervently and we waited patiently for some real benefits to emerge.

Within the two weeks, the treatment and strenuous physiotherapy were over, and I was settled once more at home, believing that something good was just about to happen and healing would come.

My younger daughter, Carrie, was to be married in the September of 1987 to a lovely "gentle giant" of a Scotsman, whom she had met at Surrey University, while he was studying psychology and she for her nursing degree. He also was a Christian believer and loved the Lord.

There was so much to do, to plan and look forward to for the wedding. I hoped so much for some improvement in my physical condition by then. During the waiting weeks of August, I received regular ministry and prayer for healing through several people from church who faithfully gave up time each week to come to my home. Praise the Lord for them!

At last the Big Day arrived. It was a wet day, unfortunately, but my daughter looked radiant beside her proud husband in his kilt in their small country church. With my camera in hand, hoping to capture the happy couple on film, I moved about and had to kneel occasionally for a special snapshot, while giving my walking stick to my husband to leave me free to move and wield the camera as well.

It wasn't until a few days later that the wonderful realization came to me: I could walk more easily with no pain, and, praise the Lord! I could put that stick away!

Feeling better by the day, I enjoyed the ability to walk normally again. All disability seemed to have gone (except for the paresthesia from the hips down, which still persisted). Occasionally my eyes were painful, but a persistent tremor through my right arm had nearly vanished. What utter bliss to have a "quiet" body! I was very excited and thanked the Lord for my healing.

My Christian GP was convinced that I had indeed received a healing, and on going back to my neurologist, I completely amazed him with the evidence of this remarkable change, and enjoyed giving him the Scripture text I had held on to in Isaiah 40:31: ". . . but those who hope in the Lord will renew their strength. They will soar on wings like eagles; they will run and not grow weary, they will walk and not be faint."

He looked at me. "I have never witnessed such a change in anybody. It must be divine intervention!" As I walked briskly to his door, I said goodbye. "You've made my day," he said.

As the weeks passed, my church and family were thrilled to see me brisk of step with more energy and strength. *Please God, may it stay like that,* I thought. During a church service, I spontaneously joined the dance group, moving easily in praise to God for His healing.

Nine beautiful weeks passed. Then, gradually, I could not deny a quickening tremor, inflammation flowing through my spine and limbs. My pace slowed and all the disability came back. After claiming divine healing and knowing such release, how could I now hobble back into church with a walking stick once again? I felt embarrassed and discouraged. I wanted to hide in the back row and not reveal I felt let down. *I must keep a low profile,* I thought.

Thankfully, I never blamed God or felt bitterness toward Him for this relapse. I only felt anger against the Enemy, Satan, as the source of pain and disease.

But once again I enjoyed the blessing of a few weeks of sun in our little apartment on Gran Canary, during the coldest of the winter weeks. I have always experienced some benefits from the dry heat, which seems to reduce pain and give me a little more mobility.

While away we had a very sad telephone call from my mother. She told me my dear father had throat cancer. He was so brave, undergoing chemotherapy and believing he would be able to make a good recovery. As the weeks progressed, his voice and body grew weaker, the weight fell off, and, eventually, he had great difficulty in swallowing and speaking. What a nightmare, particularly for my poor mother, as the demands on her grew daily.

Hector and I could do nothing but pray, believing God would take care of the situation and draw my father into knowing Him. We phoned Father every week from Gran Canary and this seemed to comfort him during this difficult time.

In January 1988, we were home again, and I was relieved to see my parents again. Mother was coping wonderfully well but needed some assistance with nursing. My father had lost four stones in weight, but he continued to smile and rarely complained. How frightened he must have felt, though, facing an uncertain future. So many questions must have arisen in his mind during the anxious months.

He was virtually unable to talk. Hector and I would sit with him to allow mother an evening out once a week, and while getting him to bed and settled, we would offer to pray for him. We were met with some hostility; he resisted any spiritual help and indicated quite firmly that we were not to pray, thank you very much!

Nevertheless, unthwarted, we tried to reach out with God's love, and I was able to just sit and hold my father's bony hand and tell him how much I loved him and cared for him.

Even through his illness he continued to be concerned for me, as we hobbled about, making jokes about sharing our walking sticks. Finally, a walking frame was required as his weight dropped to a little above six stones, and we knew it would not be long before he would have to be admitted to the MacMillan Cancer Ward.

Two weeks before he died, I felt led to write a letter to him expressing my innermost thoughts. It was a difficult letter to write. But after praying about it, I felt the Holy Spirit taking over and guiding me in my choice of words, and the thoughts flowed. I shared my concern, love, and whole testimony of the Lord's goodness in my life; what He had done on the cross, how I knew He had forgiven me; and how this precious gift of eternal life with Jesus was a free gift to my father, too, if he could accept Jesus Christ as his Lord. I placed the letter in his cardigan pocket to be read later, and we left, hoping and praying he would not cast the letter into the waste paper bin.

How difficult it was to be bold when we had consistently experienced rejection and hostility from him. Yet we knew we were being obedient to the Holy Spirit and His perfect timing. We were encouraged to think of how often we had obeyed in faith and then seen God's purposes worked out in situations later; it filled us with wonder and praise and anticipation.

Just two weeks passed, during which time peace seemed to have moved in to father's emotions. He found himself (a pathetic six stones of him) in the MacMillan Cancer Unit among caring Christians, unable to talk and with pneumonia setting in.

My family all popped into the ward to see him settled. He wanted to eat the fish and chips that were on the menu for dinner and promptly vomited it all back again.

It was the last time we saw him able to respond before he sank into a coma. Placing an arrangement of African violets with a little note expressing our love and understanding, we left him.

Arriving home and expecting a quiet evening, I surprised myself an hour later by being bowled out of my chair with a strong compulsion to telephone the hospital and ask if there was a chaplain or other clergyman available who could speak with my father.

Incredibly, the answer was yes. The husband of a nursing sister was in the hospital that evening, waiting for his wife to complete her duty before driving home together. And he was a Reverend! Of course he would pray with Father and comfort him. Once again we thanked God for His perfect timing.

Forty-eight hours later, we all (including my brothers and mother) sat with father, holding his hand. He was unconscious, but we felt sure he could hear my words.

"Jesus loves you, Father. He is the only way and the only truth."

He slipped away quietly, and I felt a wonderful peace and an assurance that I shall see him again one day. The nursing sister whose husband prayed with him comforted us with the thought that Dad was now safe with Jesus.

Through the grief and sense of loss that followed, my own symptoms became exacerbated. Once again I found myself in the neurologist's consulting room. Once again I received the steroid treatment intravenously. I must confess to feelings of conflict, as I had no choice but to allow my body to be assaulted with this form of shock treatment, while reminding myself that our bodies are the "temple of the Holy Spirit" as the Bible says. We believed that the Lord would work through the treatment.

Within a few days there was evidence of a change in my condition. All pain and inflammation vanished, and my limbs felt lighter and willing to walk again!

I was elated and praised God for the wonderful relief I experienced. My neurologist was obviously delighted as I chatted with him and kept up with his brisk pace along the hospital corridor.

"I only wish more of my patients responded in this way," he laughed. I smiled in return. Dare I hope that this time it would be permanent?

Chapter Four

Memories

SIX BEAUTIFUL WEEKS FOLLOWED, TWO OF WHICH I SPENT IN MY birth place—Jersey, the larger of the channel isles near the French coast. Oh the thrill of being able to walk with a brisk step and enjoy more stamina as we went along the familiar sunny beaches of St. Aubin, searching for cockles as I had done as a child! It was lovely to be visiting my first home and to retrace my childhood steps up the quaint, narrow roads through the old village to the little school on the hillside. St. Aubin was virtually unchanged; I recalled the lessons sometimes conducted in a small group on the grass outside in the sunshine and the daily French lessons that I was so reluctant to learn.

The hot summers I remembered—between 1940 and 1945—were in wartime, and the island of Jersey was under German occupation. I shared with Hector my memories of that time, how I belonged to a little gang keen on doing its bit for the war effort against the Nazis. We used to change the points on the railway line that ran from St. Aubin right along the coast, ferrying goods, coal, or ammunition to and from the main town of St. Helier. Or we would place large stones or other obstructions right on the track and then run and hide to watch the approaching steam engine and eagerly wait for it to topple sideways.

My father was a carpenter and builder and was often pressed into working for the Germans in repairs and maintenance.

He and my mother had a hard struggle to feed and clothe a growing family, and she sometimes stole from the Nazis' lobster pots, though she did not admit that to us at the time.

I remembered feeling hungry all the time and having little to wear on my feet; I was grateful for a heavy pair of wooden clogs (lovingly made by my father) to clump around in. My hair had to be cut short—and it frequently itched!—because we had to battle against nits and lice. How I hated to look like a boy when I longed to feel a little feminine among my three brothers.

We had our battles, but I can still picture the awful scenes of ragged and starving Poles and Russian prisoners who were forced to build roads and walls. They frequently collapsed with weakness and malnutrition. It has been recorded that many workers died while building the German underground hospital on the island, and their bodies were pushed into the foundations as so much rubble.

During the latter part of the war, the Nazis themselves were unable to find enough food and were starving. One day we were raided by two armed soldiers who ransacked our home and took what little food we had, along with our precious soap, candles, and the contents of our money boxes. A guard outside threatened to shoot us if we refused them anything. And in a nearby empty house I was appalled to find the skins of domestic animals lying in the bath; the flesh, I was told later, had been eaten by the soldiers.

As I looked at the beautiful white beaches with Hector, I remembered when they were mined and guarded by ugly bunkers and martello towers to protect the island from "allied invasion." To think that I actually dared to swim between the mines just off shore! How stupid and dangerous!

The mines also prevented Red Cross food ships from coming in. Some made it, but many were blown up. How hard it was to watch them destroyed and see them sink under the sea. It made us grateful for what food we did receive.

There were happy memories, too, from those war years—memories of the closeness and love that bound family and friends, and even compassion towards two German officers who were missing their own children and showed us kindness and respect. One gave me a beautiful china doll, which I cherished, and he often passed us a few sweets when nobody was noticing. There was a strong communal spirit, especially when we all queued up at the village bakehouse for our main meal (often consisting of seaweed!) and discussed the news of the day as we waited for our dishes. I believe my father kept us from total starvation by producing black treacle from sugar beet, churned up in a large urn. (The sight of black treacle still turns my stomach over!)

My three brothers and I had been born in a very old house, but we had moved to a larger house on the seafront, with panoramic views. The German forces thought it ideal. First they moved into a little outhouse, then they decided the whole house should be used because it afforded such an excellent viewpoint over the channel. We had to move out and found a three-story house to rent on the main coastal road overlooking St. Aubin's Bay. To us children with natural curiosity, it was an "Aladdin's Cave." Every room had old furniture with drawers of trinkets and odd mementos. We guessed the better things had been locked away and hidden. The owner was in the British Army, and he and the family had left for England, hoping to return after the war.

As I told Hector about it, I wondered if we had left the house in as good a condition as the army officer had wished.

We were wonderfully liberated in 1945. Thank God! The joyful and emotional scenes were indescribable. A huge fleet of American and British ships appeared in the bay, and numerous sailing craft and rowing boats—anything that floated—went out to greet them. I shall never forget the thrill of clambering up onto one of the ships and being given my first taste of a chocolate bar and a precious orange.

All these memories came flooding back as I talked to Hector. It was a special holiday. I was so reveling in the physical benefits of the steroid treatment and what I saw as God-given opportunities to appreciate every minute of my beloved Jersey. I was later to thank God for this brief respite and the sheer enjoyment of having a better quality of life. For the remission was not to last more than six weeks.

Again I sensed a gradual relapse into my usual neuro problems. I felt very discouraged.

I was sent to London for another scan by magnetic resonance imaging (MRI), to investigate the possibility of either multiple sclerosis or a tumor. Thankfully, no tumor was found, and there were no signs that patches of myelin, the protective covering of nerve fibers, had been destroyed in the brain, which would have indicated multiple sclerosis. There was just the continual compression of a cervical disc on my neck, which caused me no pain or discomfort. My neurologist discussed the possibility of open neck surgery, but, quite naturally, I needed assurance that there would be real benefit in having this sensitive and risky operation. There was none forthcoming.

I was left in the early months of 1989 feeling confused and frustrated. No conclusive diagnosis could be reached at this time, so my neurologist suggested that I see a neuropsychologist in the National Hospital in London. I was convinced that I was *not* being troubled by a psychological problem that caused—or contributed to—my increasing disability. But what could I lose by seeing such a specialist? I would give it a go. I had no fear or apprehension as the appointment came. Hector and I went to London the day before to stay overnight, and we even went to a West End show! I was buoyed up by prayer and my dear husband's continual support.

The following morning I found myself sitting opposite a tall, charming, handsome man in his consulting room.

"Good morning, Mrs. Vack. How do you feel?"

"Er, well, rather drunk and giddy, actually. . . ."

"Have you been drinking?"

I was rather taken aback by this response and assured him I was not in the habit of drinking so early in the morning! As he questioned me closely about all the details of my condition, I felt I was answering rather defensively, but on the whole it seemed to go quite well.

After an hour he asked me if I would be willing to be admitted into the National Hospital as a patient for about two weeks. I agreed, subject to a promise of diagnosis and intensive physiotherapy. It seemed a good opportunity to reach a conclusive diagnosis at last. How wonderful—no more misunderstandings!

During the third week of April, 1989, I unpacked my case and settled into a fifth-floor room at the hospital.

It was old and drab, and I noticed a large patch of ceiling overhead that seemed to be threatening to collapse. But as far as medical attention was concerned, I was told it was a privilege to have the finest consultants and professors about to prod and fuss over me. The top man of the team was a professor who was a leading expert on multiple sclerosis. A program of daily scans and investigations were set in motion, and I spent a great deal of time attempting great things with one large, green ball in the physiotherapy room. There were numerous other disabled patients with various neurological disorders, some looking very depressed.

I dared not leave my room because I could be called at any time to go for the promised scans. In between, I was surprised to be visited by two gentlemen who asked searching questions and filled in forms. Each day they wanted to know why I was not depressed in my condition.

My answer was always the same. I could only verify that life was good, thank the Lord; my faith was strong, and I had much to be thankful for, even in the present circumstances.

They seemed not to accept my responses, however. They gave me long questionnaires to complete, which I rather enjoyed doing, but evidently the results were far too positive for their satisfaction! I was thankful that the second man to interview me was responsive to my Christian witness and muttered words of encouragement as he left: "Great fortitude, strength . . . wonderful! . . . "Praise the Lord for that, I thought.

Day by day I underwent enormous psychological pressure. The doctor would lean over my head and say menacingly, "If six doctors all agreed that you were depressed, what would you say?"

Hardly believing what I was hearing, I answered the same each time. "But I'm not depressed and never have been!"

Beginning to realize that my replies were just not acceptable, I began to feel decidedly frustrated and intimidated, particularly when the doctor peered at me closely and said, "You are not going to like what you will hear at the end of the day!"

He quietly left the room, leaving me with fearful thoughts and confusion. I did not understand what was happening.

Thankfully, Hector spent a good deal of time with me; he stayed at the nearby Salvation Army Hostel when he could. It was so good to share with him my thoughts and fears and so necessary to unburden myself to him.

Then, on the tenth day of my stay in the London Hospital, everything happened! From ten o'clock on that particular Wednesday (with my family due to visit me from Bournemouth), I found myself undergoing a whole host of painful tests from electric conduction to electromyograms, where large needles were shoved into my muscles to record electrical activity during muscle contraction and when the muscles were at rest. The needle electrodes gave me great electric shocks, not just once, but intermittently, while the specialist watched the oscilloscope screen.

Feeling exhausted and barely alive, I arrived back in my room to find my visitors eager to see me. Ten minutes later a wheelchair arrived, and I was taken off for another test, this time for another MRI scan.

The medical staff kept me occupied all day, until by 8:30 in the evening, undergoing my second MRI scan with dye injected into my veins, my patience and endurance finally began to wane, particularly as time with my visitors had been cut short, causing me to feel disappointed and frustrated.

Oh, what a difficult day. As I lay in bed that night, I thought *"Why did all the tests have to be done on just one day?"* And I pondered the news from a neurologist whom I had not seen before. He seemed particularly astute. In his opinion there was a possibility that I may have been developing something more insidious than multiple sclerosis. I was not exactly heartened.

Nevertheless, my trust in God was strong. *He knows all things. He will never give me too much to bear,* I thought, remembering the verse in the apostle Paul's letter to the Corinthian Church: ". . . God is faithful; he will not let you be tempted beyond what you can bear. But when you are tempted, he will also provide a way out so that you can stand up under it" (1 Cor. 10:13).

Any temptation to feel angry with God receded as I reminded myself of His promises, and I was constantly reassured as I drew comfort from the Scriptures.

The twelfth day arrived—the day when I expected to hear some firm results and conclusions. But once again I was told the MS tests were all negative; the EMG was beginning to show muscle problems, but not sufficiently to give a conclusive report. Still no definite diagnosis.

My spirit fell.

I awaited the doctor's visit and his report with trepidation, fearing he would probably have a heyday with me. He had shown no sympathy or understanding so far.

I knew real fear; I washed my nervous, sweaty hands frequently during that long Friday! He finally arrived in the early evening. Hector was with me, for which I was grateful.

The doctor began his verbal report, and I became increasingly indignant until righteous anger and frustration brought me to tears.

In his opinion I had a deep, psychological root problem that would require further psychotherapy. He assured that I might well have "masked depression."

"Would you consider that euphoria is a normal reaction to your serious illness?" he questioned.

I sat there feeling utterly deflated and intimidated. To ease the pressure of the situation I thought I should have to agree with him. Could he indeed be right? Did I have a big problem underneath that I was hiding subconsciously? Maybe suppressed bitterness or depression over my divorce or the death of our baby son? Surely I had got over those traumas? If I were depressed, would I not be aware of some symptoms? Hector would be! Yet we had both been thankful that God had protected me from depression.

There was nothing to do but pray, and I knew Hector was praying too, beside me. Quietly, the Lord assured us that we should continue to acknowledge His truth. His joy and His strength in us would continue to be my witness.

Soon we were on the train, homeward bound to Bournemouth. I wished I had never undergone the whole experience at the London Hospital. My feelings and emotions were in fearful disharmony.

How could the doctor dismiss my symptoms as rooted in a psychological problem?

I wanted another opinion. In the autumn of 1988 I underwent tests at the Center of Complimentary Medicine in Southampton. Initially, I had been encouraged to go there by my physiotherapist. It seemed like a good idea, and Hector and I attended the first consultation with hopes that we would receive help for my asthma, which was an ongoing condition.

Having checked me through with electrical gauges to test for allergies and toxins, the doctor decided he was rather more interested in my major problem and asked if I would undergo a sectional electrical test. With nothing to lose and hopefully much to gain, I agreed and was wired up in a cubicle. After forty minutes, the whole of my body was mapped in graphs over sixteen sections.

Now he called Hector and me back for the results. Would he, too, say it was all psychological in origin?

In the consulting room, the doctor poured over the printouts. Hector and I sat there not knowing what to expect. Suddenly the doctor spoke.

"This is bloody horrendous! Oh, pardon me . . . What *have* you done to yourself?"

I looked at Hector. "Are you sure this isn't something that stems from my mind?" I asked the doctor cautiously.

"Oh no, Mrs. Vack. I can assure you there's no possibility of there being any psychological contribution to produce all this."

We felt a little confused and wary by his amazement as he read the graphs to the nurse. Then he turned to us and explained the graphs showed a widespread area of malfunction, and in his opinion, it was probable the toxins from the vaccinations I'd had for our Africa holiday that had affected every part of my body. This seemed to make sense, because I knew my symptoms and problems were in every area. Perhaps, at last, we had some proof of disease.

Having assessed me through his alternative medicine methods, the doctor ordered some rather frightening concoctions for treatment: an ointment consisting of cholera and salmonella, to be rubbed around my navel every other day and some drops to be taken three times a day.

I persevered with the treatment for the allotted time, well supported by praying friends in our church family who had conscientiously been alongside me throughout, but the curious medicine had no effect.

After seeing the doctor several more times, he eventually told me he thought perhaps I had MS and there was nothing more he could offer. But he was supportive in being willing to write to my doctor at the London Hospital, stating his firm opinion that there were no psychological factors involved, and he said he would also write to my family doctor.

We were no nearer a diagnosis. It was important to know what it was afflicting me, to be able to name the condition, and then to accept it. How much more anxiety and fear was produced through not knowing?

Then my arms became very weak, and my right wrist began to drop. It was time to visit my GP again. Knowing he would probably have the report from the London Hospital by now, I asked Hector to go with me. I was feeling apprehensive, even though the family doctor was a Christian and a friend, so I could expect support from him.

We sat opposite him, and within five minutes, we were made to feel uncomfortable. The report accused us of being aggressive and making a stand with stubborn obstinacy.

Dear Lord, how we longed to show the fruit of the Spirit, but how difficult when you are told to "Go and see a psychiatrist!"

Thankfully, Hector backed me up and stood by me and for what we believed, knowing that all the misunderstanding and persecution (as we saw it) from the London Hospital was beginning to batter and demoralize me. We left the surgery with our doctor's words ringing in our ears, "If you could only see that I'm right! Your problems are from a psychological root cause!"

Hurt and indignant, we knew we had to give the situation over to God. He alone understood all things. We also knew we had to find another family doctor who would accept and support me.

We prayed for guidance.

Chapter Five

Perfect Timing

SUMMER 1989—AND WITH MY EMOTIONS BATTERED AND BRUISED, I sought the Lord for His comfort and assurance.

I felt utterly isolated and unsupported medically: no GP, no physiotherapist, and no neuro support. But God was teaching me to look to *Him* for support. I had to give Him all my trust and keep my eyes firmly fixed on Him. A passage of Scripture came to mind, Romans 8:28: "And we know that in all things God works for the good of those who love him, who have been called according to His purpose." I reminded myself that He is in all things and His timing is perfect, and I thanked God for providing me with friends and family with whom I could share all my innermost conflicts and problems; the right people at the right time.

God was supplying all my needs . . . but I still needed a GP.

I got on the phone to my daughter Carrie, sharing all my confusion and asking her advice. Being in the medical business, she was soon able to recommend someone—a lady

GP who was in fact the mother of one of Carrie's old school friends. An appointment was made. The doctor was similar in age to me and greeted me with compassion and understanding. She asked if I would be able to make time for a full physical examination. I could hardly believe my ears—a doctor wanting to give me a *complete* examination! This had never happened before.

The same day, all my medical notes—and Hector's—arrived at our new GP's practice surgery by express mail! This was an unusual thing to happen in the busy health service, to say the least.

At the initial consultation, the doctor assured me brightly that she would do her best to help me get better. After the full examination her tone was different.

"I don't think I can do anything for you," she said. "There must be a lesion somewhere."

A lesion? Some kind of chemical abnormality? Everyone seemed to be guessing, but nobody knew for definite what was going on in my body. At last, though, I was under a doctor who would be honest, compassionate, and supportive. Thank you, Lord. . . .

I began to undergo physiotherapy with a lovely Christian who was in practice locally. He worked so hard to gain some strength in my floppy wrists and weak limbs, and we were pleased to see gradual improvement. Daily physiotherapy had to become a regular routine. It was quite a discipline, and I had to persevere, even when the body felt heavy and unwilling.

Although I look back on 1989 as a year of trial, amid all the misunderstandings and hurt feelings, we knew God was answering our prayers and blessing us. We had been in debt to the bank for a fairly large amount, and as the interest rate soared, we found ourselves paying more than we were earning from our few property investments. The property market was dead—nothing was moving—but buyers were found, and a disastrous financial crisis was averted.

As autumn approached, my muscles showed clear signs of wasting and my weight had dropped. Time to consult my neurologist again.

Carrie happened to be visiting us, so I asked her to accompany me to see the neurologist who examined me and noted further degeneration. Then he suggested that I be referred for consultation to clear up the matter of "psychological contribution" to the condition. But Carrie wanted to ask a few questions first.

"Will this illness shorten Mum's life, or will she get better?" she asked.

He looked thoughtful. "She won't get better, but hopefully, she might experience a 'plateau.'"

On arriving back home, we discussed with Hector the doctor's suggestion about clarifying the masked depression. I would have to see a psychiatrist, but on no account could I face seeing someone who was not on the same spiritual wavelength as Hector and me. My GP was in agreement, but locating a Christian psychiatrist was no easy matter. We trusted that the Lord would direct us to the right person.

A letter arrived in the post, giving me an appointment with a psychiatrist in November. Was he a Christian? We had no way of knowing. Dare we telephone him and ask?

I picked up the phone rather tentatively and plucked up courage to dial the number. The psychiatrist's mother answered! I explained to her the things I needed to ask her son, and she was very sympathetic, saying she was a committed Christian and she quite understood why we were asking. I arranged to phone back the following evening when he would be in. I apologized for my impertinence and asked him outright.

"Are you a Christian, doctor?"

"Well, I do believe in God and Jesus," he answered, "and I do believe in—er—the spirit of love."

Not entirely satisfied, I decided to ask him one more question.

"Do you accept the Bible as the Truth and the Word of God?"

I think he nearly fell off his chair. There was silence for a minute, and I realized he'd probably never been asked that question before, and certainly not from a patient! But he had recovered his voice. "Mrs. Vack, may I suggest we—er—continue this conversation when I am with you in your own home? I shall come for the appointment as arranged."

During the next two weeks, while waiting for the appointment, I went through mixed emotions and tried to let the Holy Spirit search my inner being and prepare me for the interview.

Odd feelings of fear crept in; questionings about past traumas and painful times . . . my divorce . . . the sudden death of my little baby . . . would I have to go through them all in detail again? I had received much prayer ministry for these past hurts and all the resentment and bitterness they had caused. I had claimed the forgiveness of Jesus and His precious, healing touch. I had felt cleansed of all the badness the traumas had left behind. Could there be anything I had overlooked, any lasting pain, something not dealt with, that would be dragged out of me as a contributory factor to my illness? I dreaded the appointment.

I tried hard to recall some conversation or some event that could be causing a deep, underlying depression. But I could find nothing. I shared my thought and fears with my Christian friends, and they prayed for me and helped me find peace in that situation.

As the appointment drew nearer, I began to actually look forward to it. The psychiatrist was to come to our bungalow early one Wednesday evening.

Praise God, I had a wonderful night's sleep on the Tuesday night! Feeling refreshed, I had a sense of expectation as I anticipated being able to witness to the grace of God in our lives. Finally there was a knock on the door at 6 P.M. Hector was praying quietly in the study as I opened the door to a tall, gentle, and softly-spoken man. We went into the lounge and sat in a relaxed attitude.

He asked me many questions, some relating to my early years and my relationship with my parents. Then he came around to the difficulties in my first marriage and on to the loss of my baby son in 1964. I was beginning to tire, but I still felt positive as he allowed me to share my faith and trust in Jesus Christ.

"If I didn't hold on to the hope I have in my Lord for the future, no doubt I *would* experience depression," I ventured.

He seemed to understand, and I sensed no resistance to my responses as he questioned me.

Then he spent a short while with Hector, and after a total of one and a half hours, he moved to terminate the interview. The time had flown by!

"Well, Mrs. Vack," he said, looking at me carefully still, "normally something comes to me after all this time, but in your case there is nothing. I can be of no help to you, because there is no big problem. Obviously, you have the normal roll-over stress due to the symptoms and physical problems that have evolved, but nothing more."

What a relief! At last my record would be cleared of references to masked depression, and my doctors would no longer be led to believe my whole neuro problem was due to a psychological cause.

It was so good to have this final assurance, and Hector and I and the doctor laughed together as we saw him out. I joked that I would call him next year for a game of tennis.

During that same year, 1989, I received a letter from *Monitor*, part of the research side of the motor neuron disease organization. They wanted to know if I would take part in their research project, conducted by a team from Brunel University in Bristol.

I wrote back saying I had not been diagnosed as suffering from motor neuron disease, but I had similar problems and would be willing to help. A detailed folder of questionnaires duly arrived.

They wanted to know a lot about me, in great detail; the whole history of my case, from when it began to the present day; how my family doctor had cooperated; the part my neurologist played. *Oh dear, I thought, should I involve them? How would they respond?*

As well as questionnaires for me to fill in, the folder included a great deal of information. There were articles on the various forms of motor neuron disease and its symptoms and details of how toxins, vaccinations, and viruses were being considered as root causes, and how the onset of the disease was often in the middle years. As I read the information, the whole picture seemed to fit. This was what was happening to me!

The most common type of motor neuron disease, I learned, was amyotrophic lateral sclerosis, better known (fortunately!) by its initials, ALS. It affects people over fifty years of age, causing weakness in the arms and hands, then weakness in the legs and wasting of the muscles. There is pain from stiffness and cramps. Diagnosis is by tests, including measurement of electrical activity in the muscles (I recognized this as the EMG I had been tested with); biopsy of a sample of tissue from the muscle, CT scanning, MRI scanning, blood tests, and myelography (x-raying the spine, corrected after an injection of a substance that would show up on the x-rays). All this was familiar to me!

I read on in sober mood, the information confirming my thoughts and fears. Physiotherapy, it said, could help reduce the level of disability, but nerve degeneration could not be slowed down. Motor neuron disease develops from affecting movement to affecting the muscles involved in swallowing and breathing, until the sufferer cannot speak or swallow at all. The outlook was not good.

If I had motor neuron disease, why had I not been told? *Maybe I should keep an open mind,* I thought, *and see how my GP responds when I ask for her cooperation and her signature for me to take part in the MND studies.*

With some apprehension, at my next appointment I cautiously placed the large folder and questionnaires in front of my doctor, explaining how I had become involved. I expected her to throw up her arms in horror. Instead, she read the details quietly and said she was willing to involve her name and the GP practice in the study of my case. Her total lack of emotion left me relieved but fearful because of the implications of her reaction. I wondered what she was thinking.

Back home, I returned the questionnaires to my dressing table and looked at myself in the mirror. I longed to know the real answers. Yes, Lord, You alone know; help me to cope with the knowledge.

⌐

December 1989 found us in a lovely new holiday apartment in the Canary Islands. We enjoyed making it a "home from home" and fit for a king! Full of light and sunshine and having superb panoramic views of the resort of Puerto Rico, it was a little oasis of peace and restoration, and we thanked God for it.

The low humidity did me good; I suffered less pain and my limbs felt less heavy and slow. These benefits were confirmed by other people living on the island—people with multiple sclerosis and polio—who also experienced relief from some symptoms. I had time to read and write, but most of all to be *still* and to let God restore my spirit. How we all need time to be in a quiet place in the midst of busy and noisy lives!

My dear mother enjoyed spending Christmas with us, and this gave us the opportunity to reach out to her with the love of Jesus and also to draw closer in our relationship with her. We longed to see her respond to His love and to come to know the Savior. We prayed for her and our relatives, and as time went by, we could see the evidence of God's power breaking down resistance to the Gospel and a change of attitude in those for whom we persevered in prayer.

In this tranquil, inspiring place, I was able to develop an old hobby—painting. I enjoyed the challenge of watercolouring and gradually made some progress. As I completed a landscape, it came to me that I could write a Scripture verse underneath the picture, something applicable that would sum up what I was trying to say in the painting. This spurred me on, and as I completed each one, I sought the Lord for the right verse. Sometimes I would wake up in the early hours of the morning saying, "Yes, that's it!" Hector had given me a calligraphy set with special pens and various inks, perfect timing for this new interest. I knew God was in control of even the smallest details of our lives, though I did not realize then how important art would be to me as my illness developed.

There was another encouragement during our sunny break in Gran Canary—the company of a Jewish couple who were tennis friends of ours from Bournemouth. He was a doctor and anesthetist of many years experience (I could not get away from doctors, it seemed!). Hector and I were listening to teaching tapes by Charles Swindoll at the time, on the Old Testament book of Nehemiah, the prophet, and Hector felt moved to ask them if they would like to borrow the tapes. They responded eagerly, and when we were all back home in Bournemouth, they invited us to spend a Sabbath evening with them. It was a beautiful privilege to be accepted by them, to share in their Jewish ceremony, and to be invited to offer up a Christian prayer after their Hebrew one.

I felt refreshed from the holiday, but I was in for more disappointment and misunderstanding from the medical profession.

Within a few days of getting back, I had to go to our GP for repeat prescriptions. I also needed to see her about some inflammatory pain in the back of my head.

Rather briskly, she passed them off as probably muscle pains and then suggested that she read a letter she had received about me from the psychiatrist.

"Oh, good," I said, remembering that the interview had gone well and that he had confirmed there was no hidden psychological problem to worry about. But something in her attitude made me stop and prepare myself for trouble. I braced myself as she read the report.

". . . and I recommend that she should seek help from me because of psychological overlay problems due to the menopause, or perhaps the trauma of late-age onset asthma, or perhaps . . ." and on it went, even suggesting that I needed antidepressants. I could hardly take it all in. It was far from the positive oral report he had given me.

And the GP, whom I had thought so sympathetic and understanding, told me that the neurologist would not see me again until I had received treatment from the psychiatrist.

Once again my emotions were in turmoil, and I felt hurt and angry. When I told Hector, he was angry, too. We had accepted what was told us earlier, and now the specialist had reversed his opinion and reported that I was mentally ill. This pill was difficult to swallow! But we had to take our pain and resentment to God and ask Him to give us peace and assurance, not overlooking that we needed to forgive those who were misjudging us. How hard it is to do that in the heat of the situation.

We reminded ourselves of what Jesus Christ went through on His way to the cross, bearing pain and scoffing, persecution and misunderstanding. We would never have to bear a fraction of what He went through for us, and since we had acknowledged Him as Savior and Lord, He would *never* leave us.

We decided to telephone the psychiatrist and discover what his true feelings were and make an appointment to see him. He told me that if I were not open to looking at psychological implications, he could not positively help me. This was a different assessment. We felt we had been misled or else had misunderstood. A new appointment was made.

I woke on Thursday morning feeling it was a day to look forward to. I was to have lunch with my mother and, later, dinner out with old friends. I rolled out of bed and suddenly fell forward, just preventing myself from hitting the bedside cabinet. *No big problem,* I thought; *the vertigo will pass.* And it did. I made a couple of telephone calls to Christian friends who weren't well, and after breakfast and our precious time of Bible reading and prayer together, I settled into my morning discipline of physiotherapy. Every morning I persevered with strengthening exercises given to me over the years, for muscles and balance. Lying on the floor, with the weight taken on my head and shoulders, something happened momentarily, and my world began to swing violently. Very carefully I dragged myself to my feet and somehow tottered into my husband's study, knowing I would find him there. Sinking into an easy chair, I began to feel very strange and drunk. "Hector . . ."

The words would not come out; something had happened to my voice.

Poor Hector looked at me in bewilderment. "What's happened, darling?"

He tried to help me to my feet, which was quite a challenge because I found that the messages from my brain, telling my feet and legs to work, somehow were not getting through. Being in charge of limbs that refused to cooperate or take my weight was frightening. Hector decided this was one for the doctor to explain.

I don't remember how we did it, but Hector got me to the surgery within half an hour. I staggered into the waiting room and promptly burst into tears! I recall a long wait, and eventually my GP's partner took me in to his consulting room and took a long, hard look at me. He examined me fully with all the usual instruments for neurological tests—the familiar pins and hammers!

"Very severe coordination problems here," he muttered. "Something major going on . . . better put through an urgent call for help."

I sat there mute while he repeatedly went through my notes, looking to see to whom I should be referred. He mentioned a name. No, not the psychiatrist again! How on earth could he help me? I tried to tell the doctor the psychiatrist had said he could not help me. Won't somebody listen?

I imagined being taken into the local mental hospital. But I was not mentally ill! I was filled with despair at that moment.

But the doctor was talking to me. The psychiatrist was not available; much in demand. Could Hector get me home? Someone would visit me there later.

With relief, I struggled out of the surgery with Hector on one side and the doctor on the other. They kept me up on my wayward legs and tried to take me out through a private door that would not yield, but we made it, and Hector drove me home and saw me back into bed again.

Everything I had looked forward to on that day had to be canceled. Gradually during the day, I found some balance again but continued to feel sick and generally unwell. I hoped I would be well enough by the weekend because my elder daughter was coming with her boyfriend.

The next day I still felt drunk but well enough to join our Jewish friends for dinner. Vertigo and periods of speech difficulty kept me quiet! Our friend, being a doctor, commented on the physical wasting he could see in my hands. He suggested that I had peripheral neuritis and the symptoms of ALS. I remembered the folder on motor neuron disease, and out came the medical books from our shelves, and once again as the symptoms were read out, I recognized them as mine.

It was a very pleasant weekend with my daughter, Sheri, and her boyfriend, Gordon. We laughed together at my "drunkenness" and discussed the ups and downs of my saga. Sheri has a degree in psychology and works with children with learning difficulties, and as Carrie has been, she has been very supportive throughout and written letters to my GP. Hector and I have been touched by their loyalty to me. In God's perfect timing, Sheri and Gordon came at the right time and were able to lift my spirits and reassure me that I was not mentally ill.

Also at that time, I was reading a book by a doctor—a psychiatrist—on "a personal exploration of multiple sclerosis." He related his own experience and offered wise counsel to sufferers who felt they were being misunderstood, especially those who were sent to a psychiatrist while waiting for a diagnosis.

I read this with interest and not a little comfort, knowing I was not alone. I decided to drop him a few lines and was surprised to receive a telephone call from him. He listened to my explanation of my situation with great sympathy. He suggested that we be wary and most definitely take a stand for the truth as we believed it.

This prepared Hector and me for our second interview with the psychiatrist. As before, he was due at six in the evening, and while waiting for him to arrive, we sat in the lounge praying together. How much we needed God's guidance; we needed the right words to say; above all, we needed His peace to come over us and for Him to overrule in the situation.

The psychiatrist was on time. Poor man, we began to feel sorry for him! He could see we were fiercely united and determined, not willing to switch our whole thinking over to considering any psychological implications in the physical condition I was suffering, nor to discuss "overlay" problems—and certainly not to accept psychotherapy to deal with them. I could see Hector was quite adamant.

I attempted to ease things a bit and move an inch in the doctor's direction. I assured him that if my normal functioning ever became disturbed, if I had a sleeping, eating, or emotional problems, I would certainly seek his help.

He seemed to understand. He said something about my problems being likened to "a ballet dancer breaking her leg" in the way of trauma.

I wanted to explain that I have only to look to our Lord and cast all my cares on Him, for He cares for me (Ps. 55:22). He is our first physician, our healer, our rock, and our comforter in times of trouble (Ps. 46:1). We must go to Him first.

The doctor finally admitted that I was not depressed. I think he was surprised. Thank you, Lord! I evidently did not fit the textbook case.

He left our home, saying, "I really think, Mrs. Vack, there is nothing I can offer you, unless—"

"No, thank you, doctor."

Chapter Six

Leaning Hard

ONCE AGAIN WE WERE ON OUR WAY FOR A THREE-WEEK BREAK IN Gran Canary. I longed for God's quiet peace in my situation. For a while it was doubtful whether I would be well enough to travel, but as the date grew nearer, my coordination problems eased enough for us to make positive plans. We never forgot to ask for God's protection before making a journey, and this time our prayers were fervent and loud as we prepared for take off from London in a terrific gale. It was a bumpy and turbulent ride as the aircraft dropped suddenly in the fierce gusts, but as we moved away from the storms on the English coast, all became tranquil.

It was like that in our little oasis on Gran Canary. Our frightened souls reached out to God for His comfort and leading, and He led us into still waters where we could hear His voice and take heed to His rebuke in areas of our lives that needed real change.

A few months before, we had decided to set things in motion for a Vaccine Damage Tribunal and were confident we would be granted a hearing in time. We were content to leave the matter with the Lord and had put it to the back of our minds while on holiday.

When we arrived home, there was the usual pile of mail waiting for us, mostly for Hector, along with a fair amount of junk mail, and a handful of letters for me.

I settled down to read my mail, when I noticed Hector was holding a large brown envelope in his hands, staring at it.

"I wonder what this could be?" he said to me. "It looks rather important."

He opened it carefully and gradually drew out the contents. All my medical notes! Sixty-eight pages in all—every letter sent from one doctor to another with all their comments (which we were not usually privileged to see), every test result, graph, and assessment. All the correspondence from the London Hospital, with what we considered to be wrong conclusions and judgments. The bad experiences and feelings of loss and misunderstanding all came flooding back.

We realized how much hard work and preparation had gone into our request for a Vaccine Damage Hearing.

I read this whole saga, up to June 1989, and was thankful my neurologist really *did* seem to be conscientious on my behalf in trying to arrive at a correct diagnosis. But I felt the reports from London had gone against me, and I had not been taken seriously. While there was suspicion of underlying psychological causes, how could the authorities believe my claim that a vaccine had damaged my nervous system?

Hector had rented a large photocopier for use in his study, so we decided to run off some copies of the paperwork, to share these normally confidential medical details with those whose support we needed.

"I know Carrie and Don would like a copy," I said. "What about our solicitor?"

The copies were duly sent off as "bedtime reading" to the people we had selected: my daughter Carrie, my physiotherapist, our solicitor, and the specialist in Southampton.

Our solicitor read the notes through with us at home one evening.

"Good gracious, these tribunals do take some convincing. . . ." he remarked, replacing the thick wad of paper on the coffee table.

"I have to say you are going to have an uphill struggle to prove anything on all these notes, but my advice is to go ahead. It will take some time, but that may be in your favor."

He gave me an understanding look, noting the marked degeneration in my condition since we had last met.

"Of course," he added, "I will do everything I can to support you in this."

It was a relief to have our solicitor's advice and to feel he was on our side. The decision to go ahead with the application for a hearing had been made prayerfully, and we asked God to search our hearts to make sure our motives were right. We hoped all the effort of preparing a case would bring about some benefit to others. With a hearing in public, perhaps my details and medical history would help the motor neuron disease research program, by offering proof that vaccine damage could be the root cause. We felt so strongly that there should be more caution in giving vaccinations; questions should be asked, and the possible side effects should be evaluated.

The fifth copy of my notes went to the motor neuron disease organization, who received them gladly and asked to be notified of my progress.

Now we had to wait for the date of the verbal hearing.

Meanwhile, I felt I should investigate the possibility of being seen by an immunologist. To make my own inquiries meant playing detective, so I put my "Sherlock Holmes" hat on and telephoned the local private hospital. Following the trail, I soon found myself in conversation with various specialists throughout Southampton hospitals. Eventually I located the receptionist for the right specialist.

"Of course, we will only see you if you are referred by your GP," she said briskly.

My heart sank. That's not very easy, I thought, having decided to keep well away from my family doctor and my neurologist because I felt they were not on my wavelength. I would have to try another route.

Through my supportive doctor in Southampton, alternative medicine came to mind. I had to go through all the details and explanations, but before long I received a precious appointment with an immunologist. *Thank you, Lord,* I thought. At last we were getting somewhere. Intensive blood tests would be taken, and if they showed an abnormal immune response or inflammation, then surely that would quash all the misinformation and misunderstanding.

As I became more assertive in my search for truth, I also realized that I was becoming more angry and indignant with all the doctors who had caused me such emotional hurt and frustration. During the early hours of the morning, I would boil over into what we came to call "my angry hour" when sleep was wasted and mental anguish took over. I poured out my troubles to Hector, and together we prayed for peace and for the Lord to heal my natural resentment and bitterness, to forgive me, and to show me how to forgive those who had hurt me.

Eventually the anticipated day arrived when I was to see the immunologist. Hector brought me breakfast in bed, and then we committed the day and its events to the Lord.

"Lord, oh please dear Lord, give the doctor wisdom and bring Your truth into this situation," Hector prayed. "Let us have no more frustration and misunderstanding. Please, Father!"

It was a bright, sunny spring day as we drove to Southampton. The cherry blossom was in bloom; there were fresh greens and dashes of brilliant yellow of gorse and broom in the open countryside of the New Forest. How we both loved the newness and color of an English spring!

Arriving at the Royal South Hants Hospital just on time for the appointment, we were directed to sit with others, and we waited patiently to be called. I was taken aside to be weighed, and much to my surprise I was not asked to remove my heavy cold-weather clothing, complete with boots! "I do hope they make allowances," I thought.

Then I was ushered into a consulting room by a lady who apologized for the absence of the consultant immunologist.

"I'm afraid he's abroad, briefly, for an international conference," she said with pleasant authority. "I do hope you won't mind me asking you some questions and examining you myself."

Do I have a choice? I wondered, but I was warming to this personality, and I willingly answered her many questions about the four-year saga, while she took numerous notes. During the physical examination, she checked me over with the usual tools for testing reflexes. Trying to find some normal sense of touch proved difficult.

She checked my eyes and they revealed their doubtful pallor. Back to the limbs. They were unwilling to move or lift, and she noted the evidence of muscle wasting.

"I must admit your condition is very bizarre, Mrs. Vack. . . . very unusual . . . You may well have an ALS problem over MS. It has been known."

Amyotrophic lateral sclerosis overlaying multiple sclerosis! I didn't know whether to laugh or cry.

"No wonder there has been so much confusion and misunderstanding," I said to her. "This isn't the first time I've been described as bizarre, either. I don't think I like being different!"

The doctor wrote some notes on bits of paper and handed them to me. "Perhaps you could now go downstairs and have some blood taken. We'll explore eight different tests, most of which will be looking at immune response."

I took the eight slips of paper and went off to find Hector. He had been enjoying a quiet nap in the waiting room. *Just like you,* I thought. We had made an early start that morning. I was glad he was with me, but poor Hector cannot stand needles and says he feels quite faint if he has to watch an injection, so he waited outside the pathology department while a large needle was inserted in my arm to take all the blood needed for the tests. I am not that brave about blood tests either, so I looked away, and convinced myself I would not feel it if I couldn't see.

I had to make another appointment, hoping the consultant would be able to see me this time so he could review my case and tell me the results of the blood tests.

We were relieved to have got this far, but impatient for the results that we were sure would clear up so much misunderstanding. My imagination began to run riot. Suppose my GP found out I had been to see an immunologist behind her back? Would she put a stop to my investigations on my own behalf? My anxious thoughts worked overtime.

"I'm sure I'll have my knuckles rapped!" I chuckled to Hector. "Do you think they'll all understand? Perhaps I'll have a chance later to explain what I'm doing and my reason for doing it."

Hector was very reassuring. "Of course you will, darling. I feel so pleased that we're beginning to get somewhere at last. When the results come through the other doctors will *have* to take you seriously." I thanked God for giving me such a strong, supportive, and understanding husband. Without him it would have been very hard to cope with all I had been through.

In our church group we were having "care" evenings, and it was at one of these that I asked the Lord to help me "hold things lightly." I didn't have anything specific in mind, but the Lord knew, and we were about to be tested in just that area. He was to teach us not to look at material things for our security.

It was April 1990, and Hector became a pensioner at the early—and active—age of sixty. We had sold our various assets the previous year and now was the time to take advice on financial schemes for pensioners. We were advised by our accountant to draw the majority of our collateral from the bank on deposit and buy an annuity pension scheme, which would in turn save tax.

"Oh dear, I don't think we're going to manage on what little is left," said Hector, rather anxiously.

"But I think there's no alternative than to tighten our belts for probably eighteen months. I'll come right in the end."

Then we both looked at each other. "The caravan!"

We remembered that we had ordered a brand new caravan to be delivered onto a beautiful site where we stayed sometimes, in the Esterel hills in the south of France.

"Oh help!" I said. "We can't possibly manage it this year."
Hector agreed. "We'll have to cancel the order."

We had looked forward so much to spending some time in May, and during the autumn, at making a holiday home of our caravan. So excited were we that we'd driven up to Northamptonshire to the manufacturer's site, to go through all the details of what we wanted, even down to the provision of a good supportive mattress—and a bidet!

Hold things lightly. . . ." We had to let it go. Funny enough, it didn't hurt as much as we thought it would. "We're beginning to learn, Lord!" we laughed.

We were still able to have our holiday in mid-May, in an old caravan, accompanied by my daughter, Carrie, and her husband, Don. It was our first holiday together as a foursome, and we hired a car and shared the enjoyment of our favorite beaches and hilltop villages. As we were all believers in the Lord Jesus Christ, we felt we had the most important thing in life in common, and we shared fellowship together as well as outings. Hector and I could not keep up with their youthful abundance of energy, so we put our feet up and soaked up the Mediterranean sun on our spacious veranda, while they went exploring or stampeding over the mountains, doing everything in top gear!

I wanted to do so much, but pain would stop me. Then as I relaxed in the sunshine and restored some energy, my mind would go to a lady I had met at the multiple sclerosis center. Her name was Cecily. She was quadriplegic and in a wheelchair, but she was the most lovely, serene person I had ever met. I knew God was in that meeting the minute I was introduced to her, because she told me she was a Christian, and I realized that the beautiful peace she exuded was witness to her newfound Christian faith and trust in Jesus Christ.

She was helpless from the neck down; her limbs were limp and wasted, and she spent all her time in a well-padded bed or a special wheelchair. I watched her persevere with writing a book, one letter at a time, using a "possum." She showed me how to use it. With its little stem held in her mouth, she could do all manner of things on a computer and could switch the television on and off. She painted using her mouth as well.

I praised her God-given gifts and her motivation and patience, thanking God for the discoveries of science and technology, without which she would be helpless.

Gradually we became firm friends, and we prayed together and encouraged one another, and I was able to support her when she went through difficult times in the hospital, when she had to cope with bedsores and immobility. She had suffered from MS for thirty years, and had been bedridden for nine. Watching my deterioration made her quite upset, but she prayed for me, and through her the Lord met my emotional needs.

Cecily taught me how to lean on God and to learn from Him in coping with disability. I thanked God I was still on my feet and retaining my independence.

Chapter Seven

Lifting the Veil

"Mrs. Vack, Doctor H. has asked to see you and will fit you into his very busy clinic."

The voice on the telephone was businesslike and efficient, and as I made an appointment to go back and see the expert immunologist at Southampton, I wondered what had come up in the results of the blood tests.

"I don't think he'd want to see me himself if the results were negative," I said to Hector.

With our hopes raised, we had to wait for the appointment. How relieved we would be if after four years we could now have some evidence of my illness being linked to an abnormal immune response to the vaccinations.

"They'll have to look at me differently!" I reasoned. *Open their eyes, Lord, that they might see!*

The day of the consultation was a beautiful, sunny day. Hector suggested we make the most of the trip down to Southampton through the New Forest, and we could perhaps stop for a bit of lunch somewhere afterwards. I'm always willing to take up the offer of a meal out, particularly the home cooking of pub lunches!

We enjoyed the freshness and color of the forest in spring, the new buds bursting into vibrant greens and golden forsythia glowing brilliantly in country gardens.

There was so much to look at. Alongside the road the foals of the New Forest ponies were trying out their wobbly legs and keeping close to their mothers as they roamed free, and there were frisky lambs out to play.

In the hospital once more, it was not long before I was standing on the scales again—boots and all—and was told to sit on a very hard seat next to a corpulent man outside the consulting room. We soon got into conversation. I had to listen to his long history of complaints—asthma, lung problems, plastic hips—but I was more interested in his comments on Dr. H. He evidently had a great deal of respect for him and had been helped over many years.

"He's a very experienced immunologist, you know; the top guy!" he assured me.

I felt slightly guilty when the door opened and I was called in first.

A smiling, genial, tall man greeted me, and I sat opposite him while he asked numerous questions and made notes as we talked. Once again I had to explain the whole history of my disease, and I made a point of suggesting the vaccinations as the root cause. He perked up at that.

"How long was it after the injections, Mrs. Vack, before you noticed symptoms?"

"Well, just three weeks after we returned from The Gambia," I replied. "My left hand became numb."

More scribbling, then he said nonchalantly, "By the way, I have to say that your blood tests were not normal."

"Really?" Surprise, surprise! I felt relieved. At last I could be believed.

He was looking at me rather carefully, gauging my response. "We shall have to take further tests and investigations, if you would be willing."

"Yes, of course. Thank you so much for your interest and time, doctor."

We shook hands, and I couldn't wait to get outside and tell Hector.

I beamed at him with some satisfaction and a sense of victory. "I'm sure the Lord is in this situation, Hector. Everything will be put right now!"

"At least we're with the right specialist," Hector agreed. We found the present circumstances encouraging and had a sense of assurance that God had all the details firmly in control.

We left the hospital and went for our promised pub lunch. Now we had to consider what action to take, if any. I knew I would have to see our GP soon. Should I write to her first and tell her what had been happening? I was sure she would understand.

My letter was open and honest, expressing how hurt and frustrated I had been after our last meeting, particularly at being labeled "psychosomatic," when the truth was I was suffering from severe inflammation. As a postscript I rather enjoyed telling her the evidence found in the blood tests.

I chastised myself for feeling angry at being misunderstood, but having waited four years for the veil to lift, I considered that my response had been natural. Now the physical evidence was clear for all to see.

I no longer had to be apologetic and explain why I had to retire to bed at 9:30 P.M., or why I had to struggle to find the strength in my legs after sitting for two hours in church! Everyone knew now why I had to be left quietly to take a siesta after lunch, for one gorgeous hour of assured peace from the telephone or visitors. It was such a blessing to be understood at last.

But how would my GP receive my letter? I gave it a few days, and then went to see her. Please, Lord, let her response be right and make her accept the evidence now!

The doctor seemed very bright and welcoming as she ushered me into her surgery.

"Hello, Mrs. Vack. How are you? Do come in."

I was on guard for any note of disapproval.

"Thank you for your letter. Do tell me what the current situation is."

Rather enjoying myself now, I launched into how I was feeling and what I was doing under yet another specialist. She seemed really interested and asked me to make sure the immunologist sent her a copy of the test results and notes. I could see she was noting the physical change in me since we last met—especially the wasting muscles in my arms and hands which were beginning to appear shrunken and wizened. I knew I looked decidedly older than my fifty-four years.

I came out of the surgery clutching yet another prescription for pain-killers and an asthma remedy, but with a lighter spirit than I had ever experienced in a doctor's surgery. At last I was being taken seriously, and I knew I could rely on the support from my GP, which I needed so badly.

Now more relaxed in my mind and emotions, I felt motivated to turn again to my developing hobby—painting watercolors. While in France I had tried to improve my skill, and I spent hours totally absorbed so that Hector had to remind me about mealtimes! I used photographs of our favorite haunts and determined to complete about six paintings every time we went away. It was far more difficult at home because of the constant interruptions.

I added a Scripture text to each and delighted in choosing which verse would be appropriate. My ability with the calligraphy pens was improving I felt, but writing the letters carefully was not an easy task with hands that were deteriorating.

In view of my output and the standard I tried to maintain, Hector suggested I could frame them at home and give them to people as presents, at Christmas, for instance.

"Do you really think they're good enough?" I asked doubtfully.

But I did as he suggested, and at Christmas I gave a number of friends and relatives carefully framed laser prints taken from the originals. They were received with enthusiasm, and I was grateful not to have to indulge in the tiring business of scouring the shops for gifts!

Somewhat encouraged by this, I approached a fellow church member who worked in a Christian video shop. Could they be sold commercially? In time, half a dozen pictures and an assortment of cards from my paintings were displayed on the shelves.

"What would you like for them?" I was asked.

"Oh, er, perhaps if I just cover my costs, I think that would be fair," I replied.

Little did I know that within a few months my pictures would be displayed in the biggest Christian book shop in Bournemouth!

Chapter Eight

In Weakness——His Strength

"MRS. VACK! MRS. VACK, CAN YOU HEAR ME? CAN YOU TELL ME what happened to you this morning?"

I peered at the white-coated doctor who was trying to help me, and I realized I was in the casualty unit of the local hospital. What a ghastly morning! I felt as though I were on a fast moving roundabout that was giving me severe balance problems and motion sickness.

All had been well the previous evening. We had spent a happy time playing a social Rummuah game with my mother and a dear friend; there was much hilarity. The collapse had come on quite suddenly that morning, with no prior warning. Dear Lord, what could be happening?

My heart, pulse, and blood pressure were taken. All satisfactory. Another doctor came alongside the bed and took some notes while I lay there longing for the room to keep still.

Eventually, they decided that nothing could be done, particularly in view of the fact that they had no specialist neurological department there. Hector was called in from the waiting area, and I staggered out to the car, feeling as if I had consumed a couple of bottles of neat whisky. Home—and back to bed. I had been through all this before not three months ago! It was a relief to be completely still and to relax. Even the slightest movement rocked my world madly.

Some hours later my GP called. She was puzzled to find me with even more severe balance and coordination problems than before.

It was only ten days before we were due to go away to France again for a summer holiday with Carrie and Don. *Dear Lord, please restore me quickly,* I prayed. I did not want to let them down.

Negative emotions, impatient frustration, and despair played on my mind. It was agony to lift my head or keep upright to eat. Hector was marvelous and understanding. I could see the way the Lord was transforming him through this trial, because where once impatience and temper would reign when difficulties arose, in their place were the fruits of the Spirit, as the Bible says: love, joy, peace, patience, kindness, goodness, faithfulness, gentleness, and self-control (Gal. 5:22–23). How blessed I was to have such a husband who was teaching me to live by the Holy Spirit, too! And, once again our church family came to the rescue with their prayer support and love. What an encouragement they were to both of us, and continue to be.

Just one week later, and thankfully feeling almost back to normality, such as it was, I popped in to see my GP for ongoing prescriptions. She greeted me with a warm smile.

I sat down and tried to collect my thoughts together with the right questions to ask. Time is so brief in the doctor's surgery, and we were always conscious of a queue of people waiting outside.

"I'm so glad you seem much better now, Mrs. Vack. You looked quite ill last week."

She seemed relaxed, unhurried; so I followed in like manner.

"Yes, thank God, I'm improving daily, and my balance is returning," I smiled back. "We're leaving for France on Saturday with Carrie and Don, and I'm very relieved I can cope with the journey."

"How did you get on with Dr. H.?" she asked. "I've received a letter from him, but I haven't got your blood results yet. He seems to feel as I do, that you don't have anything organically wrong."

She watched me closely for a response. I tried to betray no emotion at all, but I wondered what the letter said. I was beginning to feel uncomfortable with her searching eyes.

"I don't think you have really accepted your illness yet," she went on. "It would be so much better if you were able to. Do you suppose, being a strong believer, that perhaps God is trying to teach you something?"

It was an unexpected question, but I had no doubt about the answer.

"I'm sure, doctor, that the Lord has taught me a great deal. He's changed me considerably over the past four years. In fact, only last week Hector asked me if I could choose, would I want to be the fighter and active person I was four years ago, or the person I've become through the many trials over that time? I had to say I would choose to be just as I am. Certainly I've changed, in my values, my priorities . . . my trust and faith in God. His discipline has been a transforming experience."

I had in mind various biblical prophets, and how God had allowed them to suffer and to be refined in the fire as it were, knowing that "the Lord disciplines those He loves" (Heb. 12:6).

The doctor was pleased with my response.

"I don't think you were of that opinion a year ago when you joined my practice," she said, still smiling. "I'm glad you feel that way now." And she handed me my prescription, wishing me a happy holiday, and saw me out.

Only three days to our holiday, and we were having to tie up numerous loose ends to be ready on time. Then we had a telephone call from my mother, from her cliff-top house, only five minutes drive away.

"Oh Pam, I wonder if you and Hector could pop in tomorrow morning and speak to Ken? (–her companion) Come for coffee. He really needs help and someone to listen to him." She sounded apprehensive.

My immediate reaction was to think, of course, we'd be happy to speak to him, but not now! With so much to do, I was beginning to panic. I didn't think I could take any more interruptions and extra demands.

But talking it over with Hector, naturally we agreed to go. We had prayed so much for my mother, and we could see the Lord at work in her as she wanted to help and encourage her unbelieving friend, and had called on us for help. How could we refuse?

"Of course we'll go. I'm sure that's where the Lord wants us," Hector said, without hesitation.

We prayed earnestly that God would speak through us and give us an opportunity to share the gospel and encourage Ken.

I prayed silently, too, as we sat with my mother and Ken and listened to his saga of problems—a difficult financial situation, ill health, depression, and thoughts of suicide.

How can we help him, Lord?

We shared what God had done for us, the wonderful answers to prayer in Hector's difficult days in business, and the way we were sustained through the trials of illness and incapacity.

Ken listened thoughtfully and recognized his need for Jesus Christ. He asked us to pray for him.

The Holy Spirit gave us extra boldness to witness in front of Mother, knowing she was listening to every word. Only God knew what was going on in her mind at that time. I loved my mother dearly and really yearned for her salvation, but as with all of us, it would mean a willingness to make changes. Some things are so much a part of our lives that we cannot change them ourselves, but thank God, He is able to.

I was well aware of how much my mother respected our faith and our love for the church. She had obviously noted the many changes in our attitudes, values, and priorities, and, most of all, the joy and security we had in difficult times. We continued to pray for all our loved ones, as we still do.

We were so thankful that Carrie and Don shared our faith, and we looked forward to precious fellowship again during our French holiday.

It was two weeks of pure happiness. As I sat one day in the comfort of our mobile home, a severe mistral buffeted it on all sides, with gusts sweeping through the mountain ash and eucalyptus trees, I pondered on the beauty of Provence and God's blessings to us.

We had busy days, leaving at around 10 A.M. with excited anticipation for the day, driving the erratic and twisting routes through deeply-wooded mountain slopes to discover quaint old villages perched on top. The colorful Provencal houses, with pan-tiled roofs over salmon pink walls, displayed flowers in abundance in beautiful clay pots, overflowing with red and pink geraniums, gracing their doorsteps, window sills, and gateposts. Clematis, in many purples, trailed over the walls, blending with the blues of wisteria and bougainvillea. Every time we turned a corner we were presented with a painter's paradise, and the youngsters were as delighted as we were.

With the zoom lens on my camera at the ready, I stood enchanted and captivated by the scene and looked forward to the possibility of painting a copy of the photograph.

Driving through peaceful, low-classified roads, we came across expansive vineyards flourishing under the hot June sun. "I am the true vine and my Father is the gardener. . . . Remain in me, and I will remain in you. No branch can bear fruit by itself; it must remain in the vine. . . ." (John 15:1, 4). *I can do nothing without you Lord,* I thought. *Help me to rest in you so that I can bear fruit.*

Suddenly we saw a field of scarlet. "What a glorious sight, Carrie. I really must photograph that!"

Patient Hector would find somewhere nearby to park the car for a few minutes, and we would busy ourselves capturing the memorable beauty of Provence countryside on film.

"I hope this one comes out. I wonder what text I could put with it?" My mind was already going ahead to painting the watercolor on cooler days back home—fruit that would last.

They were precious days and unforgettable; sunlit days, basking on the white beaches, gently swimming in the green sea, and following the winding coastal road of Corniche D'Or.

Most precious were those times of fellowship when we prayed for one another. Carrie and Don needed the strength of prayer as their jobs (they were both in the medical profession) were so demanding, and they had little time left to be together or to be involved very much in their local community church. We thanked God for bringing us all together in that time of need as we ministered to each other.

The spiritual strength I drew from God that holiday compensated for my physical weakness, and it was wonderful to have quiet times to paint and write.

I reflected on the fact that my time was of much more value now; I offered quality time to God, used each moment with far more thought than when I was physically strong, and spent most of my time in active physical pursuits.

I sat in the caravan listening to the wind throwing everything about outside as the hot mistral blew on its way, and I pondered on the wonder of experiencing the inner core of peace that nothing outside can touch or take away. *Only God can give us that peace,* I thought. "Peace I leave with you; my peace I give you. I do not give to you as the world gives. Do not let your hearts be troubled and do not be afraid" (John 14:27).

Was I really able to hold on to that inner peace when the world conspired to throw new trials my way? I knew my troubles were not nearly over yet.

Chapter Nine

His Grace Is Sufficient

HECTOR PICKED UP THE LARGE PILE OF MAIL THAT HAD ACCUMULATED while we had been away. He sorted through the envelopes and packages and handed over the letters addressed to me.

"Oh, what have we here, darling?" he queried, waving a brown envelope with the printed address of the Appeal Tribunal.

He opened it, and I looked over the formal printed letter and accompanying copies of correspondence from my neurologist to the clerk of the Vaccine Damage Tribunal. As I read, my blood pressure began to rise.

"I don't believe it. I just don't *believe* it! What do you think of this new label, Hector? 'Conversion disorder.' What on earth is that? And what makes them think I've got it?"

I hoped Hector might offer some enlightenment.

"I've no idea what it means," Hector said, shrugging his shoulders. "I've never heard that expression before."

"Well, I don't like the sound of it, and I'm going to find out what it means," I said angrily, pushing the package to the bottom of the pile in disgust.

I've had enough of false labels and injustices, I thought, and as my indignation rose, I remembered the word of the Lord: "Blessed are you when people insult you, persecute you and falsely say all kinds of evil against you because of me. Rejoice and be glad, because great is your reward in heaven" (Matt. 5:11–12).

I did indeed feel as if I was being persecuted for Jesus's sake because I had said I was a Christian and my hope was all in Him, and without the love of God I would have succumbed to depression. Rejoice? I had to ask God for peace in this situation, but I have to confess I struggled, and I knew I would first have to discover what the label meant. I knew in my heart it wasn't going to be pleasant or even necessarily true, but I needed to get to the bottom of what they thought about me.

I picked up a dictionary and looked up the word *conversion*. It talked of change or transposition; changing in character or form; and in the religious sense of being converted in belief, changing from sinfulness to holiness. I pondered on the words and began to wonder just what the doctors were attempting to say.

Perhaps it was the consequence of my "abnormal response" to a serious disease, due to my conversion to being an evangelical Christian. Was that the "conversion" they were referring to? I was apparently far too positive and joyful, giving thanks to God for my abundant blessings! They could not understand my behavior and had to rationalize it.

I began to feel less indignant. But not only did the offending letter refer to "conversion disorder," it also recommended psychotherapy and the use of antidepressants. Not that again! It was all too much.

For more information I reached for a large medical manual that had been gathering dust on the bookshelves and was pleased to find a lengthy explanation under the heading "Psychoneurosis."

Among many terms to do with anxiety, hysteria, obsessive reaction, and compulsive behavior, I spotted the phrase "conversion reaction." *Ah ha, I am beginning to understand a bit more,* I thought. The description referred to a "flight from reality," or sometimes a confrontation with reality.

Under "conversion disorder" it said this could mean painful emotions repressed or unconsciously *converted* into physical symptoms; they could also be part of a psychiatric or organic disorder. A symptom would manifest itself as a symbolic representation of the repressed trauma. I learned that, for instance, the sufferer could be refusing to face up to guilt and avoiding responsibility, or trying to get sympathy.

It was beginning to add up; some light was filtering through, bringing me to the point where I could understand and appreciate what the medical people were postulating about my condition. My condition would appear to be, indeed, a "flight from reality" to those doctors, in their unbelief. To them, I had not truly faced the seriousness and trauma of my illness and had certainly not been able to accept it. On two occasions my GP had used the term *acceptance*: "You really must learn to *accept* your illness." They were still looking for underlying problems and thought the best treatment was psychotherapy.

I began to find peace again with new understanding of their *misunderstanding*! They had no idea of what our Lord can do in transforming our minds, responses, and attitudes in times of crisis.

I was confident, still, that the Lord had healed me of the emotional and psychological traumas in my past, and I thanked Him for giving me joy and a praising heart in spite of the continuing battle. That in itself was a miracle.

In the mail along with the Tribunal correspondence was a date for an appointment with a chiropractor, my "back man." As a doctor of chiropractic, he was well regarded and respected by the medical profession, and I was happy to listen to his honest opinions about my spondylosis and neuro condition. We sat with my recent neck x-ray displayed on the wall.

Frankly, I did my best to follow what he said, but his observations were so academic. I frequently lost track, but I valued what he had to say, particularly with regard to the possible effects of vaccine. I persuaded him to write it all down for my GP and immunologist, but forgetting a copy for me. I looked forward with anticipation to his support for my forthcoming Vaccine Damage Tribunal.

An interesting experience awaited me—an audio test at Southampton University. The immunologist had recommended it "to heave no stone unturned." It would take several hours under the care of one researcher who would test for hearing defects, Meniere's Disease, and balance problems. There was nothing to lose.

I found myself in a room within a room, with walls three feet thick and a ceiling covered with cones to make it soundproof. After answering numerous questions about balance, dizziness, and ear problems, I had to "relax" on a bed with electrodes stuck on my head and two huge headphones covering my ears.

What next! I thought anxiously.

The young audio researcher told me this particular test was for Meniere's Disease, a disorder of the inner ear caused by an increase of fluid in the canals that control balance. She said it could bring on sudden vertigo along with pain, deafness, and tinnitus.

"No, I'm positive I don't have that," I told her.

I was so surprised, and a bit cross, that I forgot her cautionary word to me: "If you find the noise too much to bear, please call for me. I shall be in the next room watching the computer screens."

She departed with a lovely smile, and I waited for something to happen.

There was the sound of a waterfall, gradually increasing; a radio being tuned; a road drill—and gunfire shots! They all burst in on my poor eardrums. Ten minutes, twenty minutes, thirty minutes, and still it continued, first in my left ear and then in my right, louder and louder, until I was quite sure I would go beserk.

This must be some kind of torture chamber, I thought. Shall I rip the equipment off or shout? Perhaps if I thump the wall she'll come in and switch everything off. I could feel panic rising in me. Three times I attempted to beat on the wall, but with no response, so instead I decided to concentrate on the Lord through the appalling din. Very difficult, but He did see me through!

Now I would have to wait for the results.

Meanwhile, I was left happily occupied with numerous orders for my watercolor prints. By mounting them properly, gilt-edged with a Scripture text underneath, I discovered how much more professional they looked.

I was only too happy to present one to someone as a gift if they could not afford to pay, if they would find the picture and verse a real source of encouragement, but I was also being shown more opportunities for selling them through commercial outlets.

After giving one away and running low on stock, I had to go into a local printer for more laser color prints to be done on the photocopier. I placed my special clear plastic folder of watercolors down on the counter and was amazed to hear comments from waiting customers. They were admiring them and asking if they could order them for themselves! Slightly embarrassed, I apologized to the proprietor for doing business on the wrong side of the counter!

"Oh, that's all right, Mrs. Vack, please carry on! Perhaps we can discuss the possibility of you doing some work for me for this shop?"

I was astonished; what a great encouragement! And I assured him I would love to paint some to order. We decided quickly that half a dozen should be displayed in the printing shop window with a notice above it: Watercolors by a local disabled artist. For sale.

How exciting. This was the third shop wanting my work, and I was humbled to think this was the only shop in Southbourne, near where we lived, to be witnessing to God's truth and promises.

Just before my fifty-fifth birthday, Carrie and Don came to stay for a few days to relax in the summer sunshine and enjoy our sea air.

"Mum," Carrie said one morning. "Why don't you consider using a wheelchair? You'd be free to do so much more."

My face dropped. I was scared of that suggestion. Far from feeling more free, I would feel I had given in.

"But you must be heartily bored with being restricted at home, just taking a short, painful walk around the block each day. With a wheelchair you'd be able to get out more," Carrie was persistent.

My son-in-law also tried to persuade me, and urged me to pray about it over the weekend.

I didn't like the idea at all. "Don't rush me into a decision; I need time to think."

The following Tuesday morning my Bible reading notes were very apt, and I thought they were just for me: "Be independent; stand on your own two feet!"

I'll do it my way, I thought. I don't want to be told what to do. And I thought of the notice in the shop window where my watercolors were displayed: . . . by a local *disabled* artist. Did I want that label? Was I ready for it and all the implications of my condition?

My thoughts were wandering; I came back to the Bible reading with a start. As I read on, I began to see that we *do* dread appearing weak or giving the impression that we have failed to cope with something—but are we really being strong when we talk in this way? Instead, I had to be strong in the Lord, to learn to humble myself and receive His grace and help, not try and be independent when it came to my relationship with my heavenly Father.

A wheelchair was placed in our car boot that very evening—on loan from some dear Christian friends. I received it with thanks, knowing in my heart the Lord's confirmation about what was the right thing to do and in awe of His timing in answering a need.

"Come on, let's go down to the sea. I'm your driver today!" Hector was ushering me into the wheelchair for my first trip.

I suppose I'd better show I'm willing, I thought, as I made myself fairly comfortable in the seat with good padding to my back. Hector checked the mechanics, and off we went along the familiar roads to the seafront. I kept my head well down and hoped we wouldn't meet anyone we knew.

We reached the promenade overlooking the golden beach, and we stopped to take in the view and sniff the refreshing sea breeze. It was a long time since I had basked in this superb scenery.

Hector was certainly a learner driver. Occasionally he would hit a pavement curb and throw me forward in the seat—or merely right out—and leave me clutching my walking stick for support, and helpless with laughter. What a funny sight we must have made, much to the amazement of passersby. By making light of the new experience and keeping a sense of humor, we were able to make the adjustment more easily and slide into a new routine. I would take out my stick more and playfully "beat" Hector with it, to hurry him on. Such a lot of responsibility and care was falling on him now, but we found it important to be able to laugh at ourselves and let the grace of God teach us.

I wondered how my mother and the rest of my family would react. Would they feel I had finally given in? Would I feel defeated if they felt that way? It wasn't long before I found out, and thank God I was prepared.

Chapter Ten

Let Go—Let God

M<small>Y MOTHER SEEMED TO ACCEPT SEEING HER DAUGHTER IN A WHEEL-</small>chair, although she never betrayed her emotions, and somehow we never managed to talk about it very much. She never commented on my changed appearance, though quite obviously, she could see the physical wasting of the muscles and the horrible boniness that made me look so much older than I was.

Thankful for the "training" with the loaned wheelchair, in time we were able to buy a chair that was perfect—light and manageable and easy for Hector to maneuver—plus a commode for the bedroom, which disguised itself brilliantly as a piece of furniture, even down to complimentary upholstery in peach dralon.

"What is life coming to!" I mused.

Learning to receive, rather than to give, was not easy. The whole idea of losing my independence filled me with alarm. The problem was I had always coped so well, keeping home and garden looking orderly and attractive, and it was frustrating not to be able to do these things anymore.

Supposing I get to the point where I'm no longer capable of cooking, dressing, even cleaning my teeth or brushing my hair? Such thoughts occasionally caused turmoil in my mind.

Take it a day at a time. "My grace is sufficient for you, for my power is made perfect in weakness" (2 Cor. 12:9). That knowledge would throw out any negativism on my part, and once again, I would know assurance and claim the promises of God for myself.

The Lord was disciplining me and training me. I learned how to prevent any negative or anxious thoughts from taking root in my mind by quickly recognizing them and redirecting my thinking on to His goodness and blessings in my life.

It actually worked, particularly in those early, wakeful hours of the morning when the Enemy was most likely to invade my thoughts! I knew I was vulnerable, and Satan would get at me through this weak spot if he could. I had to learn how to be strong "in the Lord" and "put on the full armor of God," as it says in the apostle Paul's letter to the Ephesian church: "For our struggle is not against flesh and blood . . . but against the spiritual forces of evil in the heavenly realms . . ." (Eph. 6:11–17).

I had to see the immunologist in Southampton again, and he remarked on the wasting that was now very evident.

"It looks as if your problems point to those vaccinations," he said, so I told him where we were at in our hopes for the Vaccine Damage Tribunal.

"When did you first decide to make a claim?"

"Well, at the beginning of last year, but we were turned down initially," I explained, thankful that he was sympathetic.

"We appealed later, and now we're waiting for the first oral hearing."

I was grateful for his support. "Do you mind if I ask the Tribunal to write to you for all the blood test results?"

"No, not at all," he replied. "I think perhaps we should put you through a few neurological tests—the EMG and others. You'll need to be admitted for about four to six days."

I felt I had no choice, because it was important to find out what was going on in my body and for the Tribunal to see all the evidence in writing, but I shuddered at the thought of going through the EMG tests again. In my imagination I could feel the pain of the electric shocks vibrating through every muscle. I was to be admitted to hospital in October.

It was early autumn, and Hector and I were hoping to relax in our little caravan retreat in the Esterel Hills. We wondered whether to go because internationally and politically it was a time of great fear and uncertainty, and we were not sure if it was wise to travel. Saddam Hussein, leader of Iraq, had marched his army into Kuwait and taken occupation forcibly; western hostages were being held in Iraq, and the whole of the Middle East felt under threat. British and American forces under the United Nations were gathering in vast numbers to liberate Kuwait and provide defense to Saudi Arabia, and the tabloid press were screaming about the feasibility of World War Three. We didn't want to be stranded in foreign parts. But, France seemed a safe destination, so we went.

Oh, how wonderful it was to be back in the peace of the hills and the Riviera sun. It was a delight to swim, paint, and feast on the superb French cheeses and meat pates for lunch, washed down with a little local wine. Dear Hector really indulged in his favorite flavoring, garlic Beaucoup D'Ail, with everything.

At the beginning of our third week, the expected autumn mistral arrived with force. We had never experienced anything like it. The gusty wind became a full-blown gale of forty knots, and having "battened down the hatches" and secured everything that might take flight, we took refuge inside, hoping for a quiet night, but knowing from previous experience that a mistral can be relentless for at least three days, or even a week.

"Hector, do you think we're really safe in the caravan?" I asked tentatively as the side of the mobile home shuddered.

One of the curious phenomena of the mistral was that visibility was often enhanced, giving a clear, jewel-like quality to the color of everything around. Looking at the brilliant blue sky, we were quick to notice a spiraling column of smoke rising from the distant hills at an alarming rate, and it was soon followed by great flames of ocher smoke in another direction towards St. Maxime.

"I don't like the look of that. It could be serious," I said to Hector.

"Oh, I shouldn't worry, dear. I'm sure the fire service have got it all under control."

The columns of smoke moved high into the sky and looked to be moving our way, driven by the strong winds. I was beginning to feel uneasy.

Hector didn't seem to be bothered and was thinking about our meal out, which we had been promised ourselves.

"Are you ready yet, darling?"

"Well, I don't know," I answered, anxiously watching the sky and the hills. "Perhaps we ought to stay here, just in case." I was losing some of my enthusiasm for dinner French-style on that particular night.

Great flames and thick smoke now covered most of the horizon, obliterating the wooded hills and blowing strange shapes across the coast.

Hector persuaded me it was safe to leave and go for our meal, but just in case the worst happened, I quietly removed my most precious things from the caravan—including my most recent paintings—and placed them in the car.

"Don't forget your passport, Hector," I reminded him.

We decided to take our usual route to the restaurant, through the picturesque Valescure golf course to St. Raphael.

During the meal, we discussed the fires with the waitress, hoping she might have heard what areas were affected. Doing her best, she knowing no English and we having only a little French, she suggested that possibly the golf course and Valescure were on fire! I looked at Hector in alarm.

"Don't you think we ought to go back right away?"

"No, my love, I'm sure the fire is miles away," he said reassuringly. "Let's eat and forget about it. I'm sure you must have a very 'deep-seated fear' that needs dealing with!"

I was not amused. I had suffered from nightmares involving fires; obviously one of my phobias!

We enjoyed our meal and found that the journey back by the golf course was quite normal.

But, back at the caravan we were transfixed by what we saw. The sky over the hills was bright orange as the fire progressed towards us, and eerie clouds were illuminated in the darkness. After praying for peace of mind and safety, we managed to sleep.

Early next morning we surveyed the destruction and attempted to assess how near the fire was to us. We were told that vast areas of our beloved Provence countryside had been destroyed above St. Maxime and through to Le Muy—twelve thousand hectares in all.

I remembered our trips in June with Carrie and Don and the photographs of vivid poppy fields, acres of gorgeous forests, and vineyards. They were only cherished memories now because the fire had swallowed everything it touched and left a barren landscape behind.

From our high viewpoint we watched seaplanes scooping up water as they skimmed along the surface of the waves, then flying low through the smoke to water-bomb the flames. They continued their efforts for three whole days until the smoke subsided and the sky was blue again, while across the countryside farmers and villagers evaluated how much they had lost in homes, livestock, and livelihood.

In time, and after much rain, there would be new life pushing through, young shoots and leaves sprouting from blackened trees and shrubs; and once again God's creation would be green and beautiful. It was an eloquent picture of resurrection.

Home suddenly became important to me, and I was glad to be traveling back to Bournemouth. The caravan was lovely, but it didn't have the padded bed and supportive lounge chairs that cushioned my bony parts! How cosseted we were. . . . We reminded ourselves of God's grace and goodness to us, realizing how many things we took for granted.

"Yes, it's good to be home, Hector," I said, walking around the pretty rooms, checking whether Mum had remembered to water my house plants.

The mail produced nothing special this time. I had hoped to have another appointment to find out the result of my hearing tests. But there was a letter from Jennifer Rees Larcome, testifying to God's healing of her serious illness. What a precious letter to share with my church family, and what an inspiration to see such an example of what God can do!

I was often sent joyful accounts of how people were healed and tapes of various speakers who were made "whole" again, sharing the Good News of the great Physician who could heal when medical science apparently could not.

I looked up a favorite text, Matthew 19:26: ". . . but with God all things are possible."

Lord, you know how much I long to be completely healed, too. Would it be possible? If you can heal them, why not me? But within a few days I had to go through a period of fierce testing of my faith as an insidious condition manifested itself. It would strike at the heart of my support system, my ability to communicate with others.

I would cry out to God: "Father, I didn't expect this. I cannot cope. Please help me!"

I began to feel overwhelmed with fear and anxiety, yet deep down I realized I had to let go, to let my heavenly Father take the burden. The next few weeks would test that conviction to the utmost.

Chapter Eleven

Facing the Lion

I wonder what this strange throat infection is? I THOUGHT. I had gone to answer the phone but suddenly found it difficult to produce any volume in my voice. I didn't take it seriously at first, but as a few days went by, I realized that speaking was becoming very difficult. Sunday came, and our usual church service. I had a strong singing voice, and I had always enjoyed the hymns and songs since becoming a Christian, and I felt singing was a vital part of my personal worship offering to God. I tried to sing, but instead of the usual musical notes, I was producing strange croaks and off-key shrieks. How ghastly! I had to hum instead.

The following Wednesday I whispered my problem to my Christian physiotherapist, Paul, and just broke down in frustrated tears while lying on the physio treatment bed.

"What's happening, Paul?" I rasped. "What am I going to do if I can't . . . communicate?"

He looked at me with sympathy and understanding and decided the best thing at that moment was to "lay hands" on my throat and pray. I realized he was well aware of the progressive wasting in the muscles of my arms, back, and neck, and, therefore, would not have been surprised at the development of speech problems.

But the full horror of this condition and its consequences took a while to register with me. I thought I would discuss it with my GP. She greeted me in her usual charming way, and I was grateful she seemed supportive now. I whispered as I told her what was happening. She reminded me that it was about now that I was due to be admitted for tests at the hospital in Southampton.

"I think I'd better write to your neurologist," she said, making some notes. "You realize there is nothing now that can be done for you."

I nodded as her measured words took root.

She went on, "There is only one person—and He's the best!"

Her finger was indicating upward in a gentle sweep of the hand. I nodded enthusiastically and felt encouraged at her words. We seemed to be on the same wavelength at last. Only the great Physician, the Lord Jesus Christ, could heal me. He could do it as a sovereign God, but how and when, I did not know.

Not long afterward, I was admitted to the Southampton Hospital, and on my first night I could not sleep, but instead shifted from side to side, trying to find a comfortable position on the rumpled, rubber-based sheet on the hard hospital bed. Thoughts and memories flooded into my active mind, along with the harsh reality of feeling like a victim again, allowing myself to be submitted to yet more investigation and pain.

I must be a masochist, I thought. *Dear Lord, what on earth am I doing? I mustn't think too much. I want to take hold of Your peace in these early watches of the night, and I want to sleep. But I can't sleep because of the sheet, and because someone is coughing somewhere next door to my room, and there are voices downstairs when the ambulances arrive. . . .* What a night.

I remembered a dear friend telephoning the previous day to assure me brightly that I would enjoy myself! How could I, when I was so aware now of the possibility of being investigated for the dreaded and devastating motor neuron disease. Last time I went through neurological tests it was to check for multiple sclerosis. Looking back, I had been prepared for that diagnosis; it would have been easier to accept. I knew people with MS. But MND . . . It was more of an unknown, and I feared it.

Dear Lord, I prayed, *I really hate this awful deteriorating body, the wasting, and the loss of my voice. Please give me strength to cope.* A Bible verse came into my head, God's words of assurance to Joshua: "I will never leave you or forsake you" (Josh. 1:5). I was swiftly comforted, and I went off to sleep.

In the morning I felt more positive, clinging to the hope that something could be done to clear my voice box, which was causing me increasing discomfort. How I longed to join in the singing again during a Sunday service of worship. I was thankful to be under the care of the kindly consultant physician who had made intensive immunological blood tests on visits to his outpatients' clinic, and I was cheered to have met a radiant young Christian nurse who had filled in all the lengthy admission forms when I arrived. We were able to share testimony of the goodness and faithfulness of God in our lives.

Looking about me, the room offered little comfort: plastic chairs, a metal-framed bed, and cold floor covering.

On my first evening there had been no food for me except cold leftovers, and I could not find a towel to dry myself after washing. I had to make do with small paper tissues. I was already missing home and Hector.

Be flexible, I told myself sternly. *If you could cope with wartime conditions in Jersey, you can cope with this!*

Food became better—and an ample towel was found—but the waiting around for something to happen was a trying experience. I had thought I would be safely back home after five days, but the Lord had something else in mind. I had a few lessons to learn.

I was overwhelmed by the "covering" of prayer from my church family. They sent me numerous cards and letters with expressions of love and Scripture texts that encouraged me. I was feeling very vulnerable and apprehensive about the tests, so their support prepared me for the fray.

It began. Various specialists assaulted me with scratchy implements and hammers for their neurological investigations. Three doctors put me through exactly the same ordeals. I was pricked with needles all over, bashed with a little hammer to test reflexes, and what felt like a metal knitting needle was firmly drawn from heel to toe—with no reaction. A slim torch was shone into my ears. *We have been this way before,* I thought.

Promises were made that I should see the ear, nose, and throat specialist, have a barium meal test, and I should meet the top neurologist—a professor—for his assessment. (I recognized the name and remembered he had been lecturing only the week before to my daughter and son-in-law at a rehabilitation conference in Brighton.)

As the time went by, waiting for these appointments, there was nothing much to do except talk—in my husky, muted voice—to my fellow patients in the ward and to the nurses. Some of them said they found it hard to believe that I could be joyful and positive in the face of physical uncertainty, but they didn't know Jesus the way I did! I prayed hard that it would not be long before they knew Him as Lord and Savior, too. I was not enjoying the inpatient experience, but I knew deep down that He wanted me right there at that time.

After a few days, I was moved out from my single room to release it for a dying cancer patient, and settled into the open ward, near the very noisy and busy main corridor. I longed to snatch a few quiet moments to catnap, but this was impossible, and I realized I was among seriously ill patients who required close medical care all the time. All night long there was the clatter of trolleys, buzzers going off to summon nursing staff to the beds, emergency bells, running feet, and once or twice a shrouded figure being swiftly rolled by on a bed. I could hardly look.

But above all, there was the warm activity of loving care. The first Sunday came, and I looked forward to going to the little chapel service. It was just within walking distance.

"Good morning, lovely to have you with us!" smiled a happy-looking gentleman at the entrance to the chapel.

"Thank you. I'm pleased to have made it," I replied, limping in and gladly taking a seat.

Patients filed in, some walking, but many in wheelchairs. I watched in amazement as beds were maneuvered in—evidently seriously ill patients, because they were attached to heart monitors, drips, and tubes. What an incredibly moving experience. Thank you, Lord, for bringing me here.

My eyes were particularly drawn to a lovely radiant face that stood out as she bravely sang the hymns, while she was lying attached to a heart monitor.

"*Go and say hello,*" a small voice inside me whispered. *What me, Lord? Oh, I couldn't.*

"Go on. After the service."

It was a lovely time of worship, lasting about half an hour. A doctor preached on "otherwise," Ephesians 3:16–29. When the service was over, I obediently moved along to introduce myself to the woman. Jesus just shone out of her.

"Excuse me," I said, "I felt I must come and say hello."

Her name was Ann and within a few minutes we were chatting like old friends. She was a fellow Channel Islander—born in Guernsey—and like me, she was very much leaning on the Lord and facing "lions" in her own life. She was having a heart bypass operation—her second—the next day and was fearful. We thought it was a case of "God-incidence" that we had met that morning.

Later, Hector came to see me, and I shared with him my chapel episode. We decided to pop up to the next floor to see if we could find Ann, not even knowing her surname.

We went up to the nurses' station. "Er, excuse me," I faltered, "would you have someone here by the name of Ann? She's dark and pretty and due to have a second bypass tomorrow."

"Well, let's see . . ." said an efficient-looking sister on duty. "You could mean the lady from Guernsey. She's in that ward down there." And she waved us down the corridor.

We sought Ann eagerly among the seriously ill patients amid their electrical equipment, looking for her radiant face, and then I suddenly saw her chatting to a couple of other people in the ward. Spotting me and recognizing me from the morning service, she beamed and beckoned for us to sit down near her.

"I'm so glad you've come," she said with emotion in her voice, and we realized how much she needed prayer and support for the following day. I introduced Hector.

She clasped my hand as she told us of her fear that she might not wake up after the anesthetic. So, we prayed with her for the peace and strength of Jesus to envelop her, and we asked for her healing. We thanked God for bringing us together at this critical time. When we left her, she looked radiant again with the assurance that He would not forsake her.

All the next day Hector and I thought about her and prayed for her, imagining Jesus controlling the surgeon's skillful hands. We believed, in faith, that the eventual news would be good.

Meanwhile, back in my medical ward below, I had to continue practicing to be a "patient patient." I listened to Christian radio every morning, and the words of encouragement and teaching were right on cue. "Learn to rejoice in suffering and hardship and learn to be holy. . . ." (see 1 Peter, chapter 1).

As the days passed, I boldly turned the volume up a bit, and everyone listened. A captive audience—and you could hear a pin drop! Only the Lord knew what was happening in their hearts.

Then once again I was center stage and surrounded by a large group of registrars, doctors, and student medics. I listened carefully with keen anticipation for what they had to say.

"How are you feeling, Mrs. Vack? Are the tablets making you feel less dizzy?" It was the registrar speaking.

"Well, yes," I answered. "What are these tablets, doctor, and why must I take them?"

"They're for the disorder you have in your inner ear."

He's not giving much away, I thought, but I remembered the audio tests I'd had earlier in the year.

"So you mean I have Meniere's Disease?"

"Yes, Mrs. Vack.. You require this medication continually three times a day, and I do hope it's helping you with your balance problems." He delivered that bombshell in a matter-of-fact tone, though I noticed he was watching for my response.

I sat back, considering the news. So, I have Meniere's Disease on top of everything else. Probably it was the least of my problems, I reasoned. I was feeling less giddy now and less out of balance; the severe head pain was considerably less of a problem than it had been. What's one more disease in addition to all the rest!

I began to consider this was altogether just unbelievable.

I was diagnosed already with asthma, cervical spondylosis, now Meniere's Disease, which could in time cause deafness, and, quite possibly, the biggest lion of them all, the fearful motor neuron disease.

The jigsaw was beginning to fall into place.

Chapter Twelve

No Gain Without Pain

HECTOR AND I WERE ANXIOUS ABOUT ANN. THREE DAYS AFTER HER operation, we trusted all was well and prayed for her recovery, but we wanted to see her, so up we went to her ward, and there she was looking bright, with her husband beside her.

"Hello!" she beamed. "I've come through all right. What a miracle! They can't believe how well I'm doing."

There was an enormous raised dressing from her chin right down to her chest.

Her husband had to leave at that moment, so we all prayed together with a strong sense of relief and mutual encouragement. I handed her one of my pictures with a Bible text on it: "The Lord is with me, I will not be afraid" (Ps. 118:6), and we promised to keep in touch.

I woke up early one morning and registered the fact that it was Friday. I had been in hospital twelve long days, and I wanted the tests over and done with. I felt very frustrated, alone, and tearful.

I was frustrated because I had yet to be examined by the neuro professor, and there was some uncertainty because the ward was on red alert for possible emergency admissions; beds were precious and needed urgently, and I began to feel guilty for lingering in one for so long.

Tears flowed, but they brought relief from tension. A dear nurse passing by on her early morning round with the drugs trolley came and sat on my bed and put her arms around me.

Sympathy was the last straw! In between my sobs I blurted out all my troubles and the cause of my frustration, and—bless her—she listened patiently.

"No, you don't have to give up your bed, dear. You have to stay and complete your tests and see the professor." This learned medical professor was beginning to take on the form of a mythical figure in my imagination.

Only a few hours more and there was action. A wheelchair and transport appeared to take me to another hospital for an appointment at the ear, nose, and throat clinic. I was apprehensive, knowing I was going to have a flexible tube with a telescopic lens inserted in my nose and down my throat to explore the problems with my failing voice box. I sat in the waiting area in the unfamiliar clinic, clutching the large, brown packet of my medical notes. I waited for my name to be called.

The consultant was friendly and reassuring. "This won't take long," he said. "Just a quick spray up each nostril, sniff it down, and we'll be ready for the examination in ten minutes."

I could taste the frightful mixture as it anesthetized my nose and throat—ugh! How I hated all this. But we all needed to know a few answers.

Fighting the temptation to turn and run, I talked myself into being a thoroughly cooperative patient, so that the test would be over in the quickest possible time.

Breathing rapidly, I felt the tube penetrating my nose and into my throat. Almost choking, I held on, calling quietly on the Lord for His peace.

"All over, all over. Well done," said the consultant, withdrawing the offensive instrument.

I swallowed and got my breath back.

"Is there a problem?" My voice came out as a whisper.

"Yes, I'm afraid so. The muscles of your voice box have done this," and he demonstrated two forefingers in a collapsed state. "I recommend you have speech therapy."

He showed me out to the waiting room where I sat in a daze, trying to let this awful news sink in. I had forty minutes to do nothing but think about it because I had to wait for a taxi to take me back to the General Hospital.

I turned to my favorite Psalm for comfort. "Whom have I in heaven but you? And earth has nothing I desire besides you. My flesh and my heart fail, but God is the strength of my heart and my portion forever" (Ps. 73:25–26).

I knew God would never forsake me, however deep the valley experience.

Back at the main hospital foyer, I realized that in my haste I had not taken my walking stick with me that morning, and I certainly could not struggle back to the ward unaided, especially having to carry the thick wad of notes as well.

There was a pleasant-looking woman behind the reception desk. "Excuse me," I asked her, leaning against the counter for support. "I have to get back to D2. Do you think I could be taken by wheelchair?"

She telephoned the porters and replied, "I'm sorry, dear, but you'll have to wait at least half an hour. Is that all right?"

"Well . . . I have to get back . . . my professor . . . I'm expecting to see a professor very shortly, so I really must be in my room."

I was weary and frustrated, and all I wanted was to be safe and comfortable in my bed again. I was upset with myself not being able to manage the eight-minute walk without my stick.

"Shall I see if a nurse from your ward could collect you, then?" she asked, picking up the telephone again.

Within five minutes my favorite staff nurse arrived, and with a huge grin, she suggested we pop quickly into a foyer shop that was displaying attractive, woolly winter clothes. At first irritated by this request and the extra delay, I was soon amused at the situation. *If you could see me now, Hector,* I thought, *straight out of an awful examination—and going shopping!* The nurse cleared a path through the crowds of people scurrying in different directions near the main entrance, and, still clutching my notes firmly, I clung on to her while we went into the shop and stood by the colorful racks.

Feeling I deserved to go a little berserk and spoil myself, I decided to grab a lovely embroidered sweater. *Just right with black trousers,* I thought, and she secured it for me.

Thank you, Lord. What a lovely pick-me-up—just when I needed it!

Arriving back at my medical ward and flopping down into a chair, I was offered a cup of coffee. Glancing around, I noticed a stranger talking to my consultant. I perked up as the consultant walked over towards me.

"Mrs. Vack, Professor M. is here, and he would like to examine you."

I immediately liked the look of the gentleman.

The brown curtains were drawn around my bed, and I prepared myself to go through yet another physical examination. But, the professor didn't come immediately. I could just see him, pouring over my notes and discussing something. Then, he finally appeared.

"I'm pleased to meet you, Mrs. Vack. I understand you have toxin problems." He sat down on my bed. "Oh dear, you do have a wasting problem." He expertly assessed my bony limbs, shoulders, and back, tapping and prodding me all over with the familiar neurological tools of the trade.

"Have you been anywhere near crop spraying or perhaps nuclear waste dumping?"

I flinched and tried not to smile. "No, I believe the problem stems from vaccinations," I told him.

I knew he wanted to explore other possibilities, and his suggestions made me wonder what on earth those blood tests had revealed.

Finally, the examination was over. The professor left, and my consultant came over to my bed and sat down to discuss whether or not I could stay in hospital to undergo further tests recommended by this not-so-mythical professor of neurology. I was relieved that a final diagnosis could not be far off now, and I thanked God for the privilege of being under the professor and a respected team of experts. The Lord is good and His ways are perfect.

I knew deep down that all I was going through was for my own good, ultimately, though I longed to be at home with Hector, planning and preparing for a family Christmas.

To my delight, since there were six "spare" days to wait for my next electrical tests, I was asked to become an outpatient instead. But, before I left for home, I wanted to speak to the consultant to ask him a straight question.

"Do I have motor neuron disease?"

I watched for his reaction, and seeing little, I decided to press on boldly. "I do have motor problems. . . ."

He nodded, but there was no further comment, and I knew I would have to be content without a firm diagnosis until he was 100 percent sure. Nevertheless, I left that day feeling reassured, peaceful, and supported, happy that they would find out more from further monitoring and the necessary examinations and tests, and that everything would be done to relieve my difficulties and pain and ease the way through the progressive disability that quite likely lay ahead.

Time to go home! Poor Hector made about four trips from my room to the car, helped by my mother, carrying my special mattress from home, along with my pillow and my own bath mat and suitcase, then plants, board games, and arms full of get-well cards and letters.

We were also handed all my latest medical notes, which we later found to be useful and specific evidence of my condition, including all the results from the electric nerve tests on the motor and sensory nerves, showing all the abnormalities.

The professor's letter was even more interesting. Seeing all the findings in black and white before me was like reading a horror story. I found myself detached from the reality of it, as if I was reading someone else's case history. Perhaps my mind was exercising a defense mechanism to protect me from the impact of the truth, which was awful to contemplate.

He made reference to all the marked wasting through my arms, hands, shoulders, and hips; also the loss of sensation over a wide area. Having made a thorough examination, he considered that I had a generalized sensory and motor neuropathy, together with upper motor neuron signs, especially regarding my legs, and he went on to describe the various signs.

One sentence stood out and troubled me: "I am concerned at the tempo of recent changes." *Oh dear,* I thought, *I don't like that at all.* I wanted to enjoy Christmas, but I wondered what the New Year would have in store for me? Surely, surely the Lord would not forsake me? I had gained so much from Him so far, but how long, oh Lord, must I wait for Your healing touch? How long? . . .

Chapter Thirteen

His Healing Touch

THE CHRISTMAS PERIOD WAS TAKEN UP, AS EVERY YEAR, WITH BUYING gifts and wrapping them, posting cards, and preparing for the family get-together. This time I did not have to do all the cooking!

One day we had an unexpected telephone call.

"Say, is that you, Pam? Is your apartment free right now, or are you gonna use it?"

It was the warm American voice of a friend of ours, Ray, an evangelical minister who ran a missionary college in Gran Canary. We had decided not to travel for our usual break in the sun that winter, so our holiday home was free. I wondered what he had in mind.

"I just kinda wondered if you'd let some missionaries use it for a while? They've come from Mauritania and there's no way they can go back, so I guess they're homeless."

"Oh, Ray," I said, "how terrible for them. Yes, of course they must use our apartment. But hold on, here's Hector."

And I passed the phone over to my husband to sort out the details. I knew he'd agree with me. We had evidently made the right decision about not going, because the Lord knew these people needed somewhere to stay, and He had made the arrangements for them! We felt humbled to be used in this way for His purposes, and we thanked God for the warmth and comfort of our lovely home and the chance to share what we had.

I was receiving much-needed prayer ministry at this time. When there was so much going on in the world that needed prayer—the Gulf War, for instance—I felt unworthy of the attention.

One of my prayer partners, Pauline, soon put my mind at rest. "Don't you think, Pam" she said, "that God wants your healing as well as being more than able to intervene in world affairs?"

I had to agree and welcomed the ministry. As we talked about stumbling blocks that could be hindering my healing, I discovered there were still areas of guilt to be dealt with. I was still blaming myself for the death of my baby and for my failed marriage, and I was also limiting God's blessing by not being open for Him to work in me.

I tried to explain to my three prayer warriors.

"Can't you understand that I've felt such gratitude and thanksgiving for His grace and joy—every day—because He's protected my mind and my spirit! It's been such a testing time, but I've had no depression, no self-pity, no long periods of mourning for the loss of my health. I haven't given in! The Lord has been with me every step of the way; so what more could I want?"

I was quite content to continue as I was, but they asked why I could not accept that God wanted me *whole* and *completely healed* again.

Thinking about it, yes, I had to agree that I wanted to reach the point where I could believe that our Lord could—in an instant—vanquish the roaring lion that was seeking to devour my body and could work a miracle of recovery. But, it was so difficult to believe that, especially in the face of so much evidence of destruction! I could see that my sisters in the Lord were not satisfied with listening to my praising heart, and they wanted to know what was going on underneath!

After much probing and prayer, I had to admit the Lord was giving them sharp discernment, and I found myself facing the reality of my situation head on.

"Give your underlying emotions to the Lord," they encouraged. "Ask Him why He hasn't healed you. Tell Him how frustrated you are."

I had to take a long, hard look at myself, and I didn't like what I saw. I realized I had been striving and pushing myself in my own strength, not daring to let the Lord down. I was keeping up my Christian appearances, thinking I was honoring God by so doing. No wonder so many friends around me thought I was coping so well, always looking bright and chirpy, because I dare not admit to an occasional struggle.

Eventually honest tears flowed and my grief poured out.

"Lord, I'm fed up with this dead and numb body! I hate it; I loathe the weakness and wasting and all that's happening. Lord, I want my voice back! I want to sing to you again. . . ." I was quite broken. "Father, I mourn for the strength and vitality I had on the tennis court—please, *please* bring it back again. It used to be such fun . . . only a few years ago, Lord . . . running and jumping and hitting a tennis ball. I rejoiced in the health and energy you gave me. Oh, why, Lord.? . . ."

I became aware of Hector standing behind me weeping too. I felt a mixture of emotions; I loved him so much

I had wanted to keep from him these tears of mourning and my innermost fears for the future. Had it been wrong to hold back, to stop short of being open and honest with each other? Had we missed out on blessings from God because we had not shared how we were feeling when we prayed together?

We admitted to dear Pauline, Tina, and Gill, who patiently ministered to us, that we had felt guilty praying for ourselves.

Tina had some advice for us: "I want you to spend one morning a week just giving everything to the Lord and praying honestly for yourselves."

"Yes, we'll gladly do that," Hector and I assured her, "and we won't feel guilty about it!"

There was little doubt in my mind what the Lord was saying to me by His Spirit. I was undergoing a personal, spiritual struggle.

Having always been someone who valued her independence and ability to cope, I suddenly found everything put into reverse: "for when I am weak, then I am strong." I recalled from the words of the apostle Paul (1 Cor. 12:10). Dare I admit to being weak and vulnerable, needing help and assistance, even losing my independence? I knew in my heart that was where the Lord wanted me—totally dependent on Him, drawing from His resources and strength.

I knew the Scriptures so well in theory: "I can do everything through Him who gives me strength." (Phil. 4:13). Was I prepared to put that into practice?

I made a new pact with the Lord and with patient Hector.

"From now on," I said, "I'm going to be really honest and let you know when I need prayer, when I have to say no to going to meetings, or when I have to turn down going to see friends for coffee or tea. And I won't feel I have to justify saying no."

The new assertive me was going to find it hard—and I knew I had to rely completely on the Lord to give me the courage to be open. I had always been concerned not to upset people and would frequently agree to doing things against my better judgment, rationalizing with myself, "They don't understand where I'm at because I still look well, so I'd better go!"

I wondered how this new frankness and honesty was going to be received by my family and friends. Perhaps, with no barriers of pretense now, they would really understand and see me in weakness rather than in strength.

I admitted to Hector and the girls that the thought of losing my independence was very frightening, and I knew in my heart that great battles lay ahead. Already, even the little task of dusting our single-story home exhausted me, and I was finding it hard to ask Hector for help. Deterioration in my condition was obvious to everyone: my voice was becoming increasingly weaker, and the first appointment for speech therapy was near; day by day it was getting more difficult to support my weight, and I would soon need a prop, or neck collar.

Step by step I knew my will was being broken and crushed—very painful! But, in our Lord's mercy and love He gave me a desire for the sweet aroma of Jesus to permeate my will while He rebuilt me in His way, reshaping, re-molding me as I yielded more to Him and His purpose through this trial.

And at last I am beginning to feel like a workable piece of clay in His hands. I long for Him to shape and refine me into something beautiful—a vessel that can be wonderfully used to His glory.

I have a long way to go, but meanwhile I take hold of His promises: "Blessed is the man who perseveres under trial, because when he has stood the test, he will receive the crown of life that God has promised to those who love him" (James 1:12).

While writing this, I have meditated on the wisdom of words spoken by a Christian teacher on Trans World Radio: "Our main business is not to see what lies dimly in the distance, but to do what lies clearly at hand."

Lord, help me to do just that.

Words were given to me by the Holy Spirit that I had to write down. I share them here.

YET WILL I PRAISE HIM

Even though I cannot sing,
I've a song in my heart,
Rising up in my Spirit to Thee,
Even though my frame is weak,
diseased in every part,
Your unfailing love of that I'll speak,
embracing all of me.

Hope arising, joy through less,
Abundant grace; His life it cost,
My sins forgiven, He set me free,
All to show His love for me,
Even though the body wastes,
The enemy has not won,
God streams His healing; restoring, sealing,
me undeserved in His love.

Jesus is Lord, His power revealing,
in His name—we've overcome,
And, yet, dear Lord, the road is hard,

> The valleys deep; the mountains steep,
> Teach me Your truth and promises too,
> Dear Father help me trust in You.

Therefore, we do not lose heart. Though outwardly we are wasting away, yet inwardly we are being renewed day by day. For our light and momentary troubles are achieving for us an eternal glory that far outweighs them all. So we fix our eyes not on what is seen, but on what is unseen. For what is seen is temporary, but what is unseen is eternal. (2 Cor 4:16–18)

To which I can only add, Hallelujah!

Chapter Fourteen

New Beginnings

"HECTOR, DO YOU THINK IT WOULD BE A GOOD IDEA TO MOVE TO something smaller and more manageable?" I asked. "I'm finding these stairs very exhausting and hard to climb. How do you feel about looking for a bungalow or a cottage in the country?"

I watched my husband's face carefully for a response.

"Well, there's no harm in just looking, I suppose," he replied cautiously.

Having lived in our beautiful Spanish-style house for fourteen very happy years and knowing God's blessing upon us, it was alien to us both to even consider a move. I knew the process would be totally exhausting. Experts rate a move of a household to be as stressful as a divorce (which I wasn't contemplating!). Nevertheless, I would not be put off as I looked to the future benefits in the long term for us both.

We had spotted an old cottage for sale at the end of a lane, overlooking open countryside a few miles out into an attractive rural area, and not too far from mother, friends, and church. As we peered at it from all angles, the seeds of interest began to germinate, and we decided to act and actually view the property.

One telephone call later, an appointment was made, and here we were, eager to look it over and hoping that everything would be ideal for both of us.

The views were perfect. But, we soon discovered a disadvantage—the local airport. The cottage was right under the flight path.

"Wow, that one was close!" I gasped, as we watched the huge body of an airplane roar over the roof top, and I had to resist the urge to duck.

Sadly, the stairs were steep and the general layout just wasn't ideal, so we left the property with the urge to view more homes for sale and seek the place that we believed the Lord had reserved for us.

The big decision was made; a For Sale board was placed firmly in our garden near the gate. It was July and the housing market was very depressed due to economic recession. Cash buyers were like gold and hard to find, but I strongly believed God was in control, as we had prayerfully given the whole situation to Him, and we believed He would bring a buyer along in good time.

The first Sunday approached and it could not have been wetter. The telephone rang, and we were informed that our first "viewers" were on their way. The house looked very presentable inside, but the dull, dreary conditions outside were hardly conducive to showing it off at its best.

The doorbell rang, and with mixed feelings, we answered it and were suddenly greeted and introduced to an exuberant Spanish family, plus their own Spanish-to-English interpreter. Later, we realized just how necessary and helpful she would be in negotiations. Hector and I were amused to watch the Spanish gentleman head for the lounge and immediately drop to his knees on the floor with a tape measure. We could see he meant business, and, thankfully, we heard an occasional "*Si, si,*" and began to feel a little encouraged.

We didn't know then that the grand, ornately-carved furniture he intended bringing in would require a very large lounge, or as he put it, "a salon." He seemed satisfied and was sufficiently interested to make an offer before leaving. It was well below our asking price, but we were filled with anticipation. Within the hour, the telephone rang and negotiations began in real earnest. Finally, an acceptable figure was offered, and we agreed.

Our search for a new home for ourselves began.

"Hector, how do you feel about living on the other side of town—somewhere within walking distance of those beautiful beaches and wooded chines?"

"Yes, I think that'd be a good idea. We've considered it before, you remember, but perhaps now's the right time." Hector remembered our wishes many years ago when the schooling of my girls determined where we lived.

Gradually, a number of estate agents busied themselves searching among a large number of bungalows for sale, enticing us to buy. Sheaves of property details arrived by post each morning, and we would take a handful and ring for an appointment to view them, with great enthusiasm. We decided to place an offer on a chalet bungalow that seemed to offer the best facilities and was the nearest to our desires, although, after a second examination, we discovered it needed a lot of work and money spent on it. Settling up an account for new windows and a kitchen, we were stretching ourselves financially. Nevertheless, we made a firm offer in faith and waited for the response from the existing owners.

Meanwhile, we continued viewing other areas, and I began to feel exhausted trailing around property after property.

I complained to Hector. "Why do we have to waste everybody's time and energy looking into every nook and cranny—even the garage space—when you know perfectly well the bungalow's a 'miss'?" I hoped he'd give me a good reason.

"Well, we've got to show some interest," Hector rationalized. "After all, they've made a special effort to show us around the property."

I began to feel increasingly frustrated. It had seemed so right to move, and we had seen so many properties, but so few that were suitable for us. "Please, Lord, You know where You want us to live. Will You show us?"

Ideally, we hoped to find a home in a quiet and flat situation with a reasonably-sized lounge, a good kitchen, and two or three bedrooms. And, if we were really fortunate, it would be near the sea so Hector could enjoy his daily walk . . .

We discovered a property overlooking a golf course, an executor's sale and beautifully decorated. Facing a southerly situation, the front was bathed in sunlight—but once again there was a steep staircase, and a north-facing main garden. Not ideal, but I was beginning to get desperate, especially since our buyers were pressing us to move out!

Once again we made a firm offer. Now we had two offers in the pipeline, and we waited for some response from the estate agents. Silence. Not even a phone call. So, having exhausted all the possibilities on two sides of Bournemouth, it seemed right to begin a search to the east of the town. More details and more appointments!

We gazed with increasing interest one morning as we sipped our coffee, at the description of one particular bungalow. It had caught our eye because there was a special note: Well recommended. Somehow the photograph of the lovely property created in us a real sense of expectation, and the asking price was more within our reach.

"Oh, Hector, please let's go and see it this morning," I pleaded.

A phone call later and we were on our way. First, we had to go through the motions of viewing two other bungalows previously booked, and I was beginning to run out of energy, but as we approached the "well-recommended" bungalow, we had a sense that this was the home the Lord had chosen for us. We gazed admiringly at the attractive frontage, partly clad with Purbeck stone, and the large picture windows, and through a welcoming porch. Before long we were utterly convinced. There on the walls inside were plaques featuring Scripture texts, and we sensed the presence of God and His blessing upon a home that we found out was occupied by two lovely Christians.

From the large, warm hallway, we looked in to a sunlit lounge, and it got better! Beyond was a superb sun lounge and an unbelievably perfect patio and garden. We gazed in wonderment and incredulity, both inwardly praying, *Dear Lord, is this where You want us?*

We were led into the natural garden, with a new orchard of superb fruit trees—apple, plum, and pear—along a small path passing through a copse, and on to a meadow beyond the garden. I couldn't believe my eyes as I gazed past a small bridge, over a stream toward a beautiful stretch of smooth water that formed a lake. Contented ducks, mallards, and moor hens moved here and there in search of food. A shingled path skirted the water and disappeared into the distance.

Two or three wooden seats perched invitingly near the water's edge, and as far as the eye could see there were meadows and trees and wooded copse—an artist's paradise. We wondered if it could be ours.

An offer was made, and after further negotiations, we all arrived at an acceptable transaction. How we thanked and praised our Lord! He knew just where He would have us live and had taken us from one side of town to the other. We had never considered moving to this area, but we believed God in His wisdom had closed the door on our previous offers and prepared the way for us.

It was late summer, time to settle in before the long, dark days of winter approached. After five hectic weeks of sorting and clearing out and deciding which pieces of antique furniture had to go to auction, we found ourselves on the road, filled with happy anticipation.

"Do you know we're homeless?" Hector joked, as we were halfway between the two homes. We were experiencing a mixture of emotions such as joy, expectation, and a new hope for the future, a new beginning, with a tinge of uncertainty. Personally, I was grateful that I could now live on one floor instead of having to climb stairs.

The removal day went well, though I was totally exhausted with no opportunity to rest. My eighty-year-old mother was happy to help, busying herself in the kitchen, putting away equipment and foodstuffs. By the evening we were only too happy to fall into bed and didn't mind living among cardboard boxes and packages for a few days.

We chose the bedroom with superb views of the garden and glimpses of the lake beyond. What a joy it was to wake up and draw the curtains on that view every morning!

We felt we were suddenly living right out in the countryside; we were not overlooked, but enjoyed open views of God's wonderful creation, filled with the changing colors as each season came. Indeed, it was an artist's paradise affording numerous opportunities and fresh inspiration for new pictures to paint. I ventured around the lake, frequently capturing the changing reflection and color of the water. As the autumn drew in, the trees were clothed in a spectacular variety of golden amber, rust, and red-brown, and my camera was very much in use capturing all its beauty.

My watercolor pictures were well received through the Disabled Artists' Society, and I was encouraged by the frequent sales of my work during various exhibitions held in the center of a busy shopping precinct and in a number of top hotel lounges in and around Bournemouth. My spare time was spent happily painting and attempting the challenge of new subjects. As a member of the Meniere's Society, I received details in their newsletter of a competition to paint a Christmas card. I submitted a small snow scene, complete with picturesque church and a river flanked by wintry trees. I waited in anticipation, and a letter came informing me I had won joint first prize! Better still, my picture was chosen to go into print for the Meniere's national Christmas card. Thank you, Lord! What an encouragement to persevere and move on to better things. I was so grateful to God for the gifts and grace He bestows on us.

During our first six months in our lovely new home, we enjoyed getting to know our neighbors over many tea times, while we sampled the results of Hector's new hobby—baking cakes. He relished taking over the kitchen for a day and keeping me out!

All our friends arrived expecting to be offered a whole variety of regional culinary specialties and left singing Hector's praises. Even the Multiple Sclerosis Society (where I continue to receive physiotherapy) looks forward to receiving Hector's famous lemon sponge and banana bread to be sold in aid of their funds, and to be eaten at coffee break. "Here's our goodie boy!" my physiotherapist hails him.

During late autumn, I received a phone call from Vincent, who runs the Disabled Artists' Society, asking me if I would take part in a film about the Langside School for children with cerebral palsy.

"The crew could be with you about 8 P.M. on Wednesday night," he said, and I agreed to be involved. Vincent assured me the film would be for television and Meridian TV was already interested.

How exciting, I thought. Life was certainly not dull. I pondered on what they might interview me about, and what I would say. *I hope I have a good day and don't get tired out before they come,* I thought, knowing I am not at my best in the evenings.

Thankfully, on that particular Wednesday I enjoyed one of my better days (thank You, Lord!), and we welcomed the film crew and Vincent at the time arranged. After much discussion over numerous cups of tea, it was decided that I would use my favorite padded chair for the interview and my art studio/bedroom for one or two shots of me painting. A busy two hours followed, with our normally quiet bungalow full to bursting point with at least nine crew members and technical equipment everywhere. But, it was good to have an opportunity to share my faith and our hope in the Lord. *Please use it for Your glory,* I prayed silently. Eventually, I received my own personal video copy, which was then shared with friends and church family.

Hector and I were pleased to see that the whole theme covering the school for children disabled by cerebral palsy was like a prayer to God and thanksgiving for His blessings within various situations.

I cringed a bit when I saw the video, though. The two other disabled artists in it seemed to come over so much better than I, and I felt some embarrassment watching myself.

Did I really sound like that? My voice was breathy and low because of my difficulties in finding sufficient strength and volume to sound the words. But the whole event had been very enjoyable, and I felt it was a privilege to be asked to take part. For a quadriplegic friend of mine, Cecily, it had been a special day. She was filmed in her nursing home. We both found it a source of encouragement to carry on painting through the Disabled Artists' Society.

With so many positive blessings and new opportunities opening up, we were not prepared to experience one more "thorn in the flesh."

To win my case for a Vaccine Appeal Tribunal hearing, we were advised by a local medical solicitor that we should attempt to win support from a neurological consultant in London. Eventually, we received a letter back to inform us that the consultant had read all my notes carefully and considered—without seeing me—that I stood not the remotest chance of making a claim for vaccine damage.

We asked the consultant to recommend a colleague for a second opinion, hoping that another specialist might hold a different—and supportive—opinion. In retrospect, we realized how foolish we were to ask for a colleague, rather than seek an independent view for ourselves.

An appointment was made to see a consultant neurologist in a London hospital. Hector and I set off with much expectation, ready for an hour's consultation. Our hopes were high as we were received graciously and led into a consulting room.

All that followed led me to feel somewhat disturbed as he ventured for all of fifty minutes to extract from me a complete family history, even asking about my schooling, exam results, and career. I began to wonder if he wanted to know if my grandmother had suffered from ingrown toenails!

Finally, looking at my watch and realizing our one hour was nearly up, I decided to be assertive.

"Er, forgive me for asking, but are you going to examine me?"

"Of course, Mrs. Vack. Would you care to come over here?"

I felt quite relieved as he ushered me to the medical examination couch. A brief and cursory look-over followed as he concentrated on discovering my sensory level using needles. Sadly, he did not take the time to examine my wasting back, shoulders, and upper trunk, but we bid him farewell and went on our way back home to Bournemouth, hopeful that the support we badly needed would be forthcoming from this man.

Every morning during the weeks that followed we watched eagerly for the post to arrive. Surely our good news and support would come soon?

Eventually, a large, buff envelope bearing our solicitor's name arrived. We opened it keenly and felt our hopes sag as we read the covering letter. He was full of apologies for the contents of the report and the fee requested. We read on.

Page after page of carefully copied notes were presented as part of the report—details taken from an earlier medical report, including all the misunderstandings and confusion that had caused me so much hurt and confusion. He did not support our case for a Vaccine Damage hearing.

Some days later, when I was re-reading the notes, it dawned on me why this particular consultant had adopted such a view.

"Of course!" I cried out. "It's my fault, Hector. I've just realized he had only half of my medical reports; there's a lot missing. How could he have come to any other conclusion?"

If only I had made sure that he had in his possession the recent muscle biopsy test result, which showed a number of abnormalities, and all the clinical photographs showing the *evidence* of changes brought about by my muscle wasting over recent years.

The real sting in the tail was the bill—nearly a thousand pounds!

We both felt a deep sense of disappointment and anger. It seemed such an exorbitant fee for so little work. We took all our feelings and emotions to God, praying together. It had seemed so right to proceed with our claim—or at least gain a hearing—but all our efforts had come to nothing.

After all the years of preparing and pressing for a case, we now felt drained of emotional energy, but the Lord gave us peace—and a decision. We would withdraw our application. With lighter, united hearts, we sat down to write a letter.

While in the consulting room in London, we had been given the opportunity to talk about our faith. Interestingly, the neurologist had made a special note as we shared what Jesus Christ meant to us in our daily life. I sensed perhaps he was disturbed at being face-to-face with two outspoken evangelical Christians. Definitely a "conversion disorder"!

A Bible passage came to my mind: Matthew 5:11: "Blessed are you when people insult you, persecute you and falsely say all kinds of evil against you because of me. . . ."

God's word is so very precious and timely in healing our damaged emotions; He brings peace and the ability to forgive those who cause us heartache and misunderstanding. And He enables us to learn to respond in a godly way, with the desire to please Him. I found it hard, an ongoing battle with the old self.

I look back to the time when God allowed my good health to be snatched away, and I do not feel bitter or resentful. I can testify to His abundant grace and can give Him the glory for all that He has done and is continuing to do within me by His Spirit.

I continue to be monitored closely by my neuro-professor and other specialists every six months. I sense the frustration of my GP, who refers to me as a "rare beast," and other experts who are confounded by the rarity of this particular neurological disease that gives rise to many uncertainties. I share with many others concern for the future, but it is good to be reminded that everything is under God's control. He understands totally, and I believe He has allowed it for my own good and is able to withdraw it, if He is willing.

I know I am having to learn to trust our Lord totally as my bodily frame continues to weaken and waste and causes me so much inflammatory pain. My hope in Jesus has not diminished but grown brighter than ever before as I learn to take one day at a time and remember to thank Him in every situation, whatever may present itself in the future. As the apostle Paul wrote so aptly: ". . . he (God) said to me 'My grace is sufficient for you, for my power is made perfect in weakness. . . .' For when I am weak, then I am strong" (2 Cor. 12:9–10).

What an incredible promise! I feel so undeservedly loved and blessed.

Since completing this manuscript, Pamela has been finally diagnosed as suffering from atypical ALS, otherwise known as motor neuron disease.

To order additional copies of

Facing
the Lion

Have your credit card ready and call

(877) 421-READ (7323)

or send $9.95 each plus
Shipping & Handling*

Your choice: $3.95 - USPS 1st Class
$2.95 - USPS Book Rate

to

WinePress Publishing
PO Box 428
Enumclaw, WA 98022

www.winepresspub.com

* Add $1.00 S&H for each additional book ordered.